Write Your Way to a 6-Figure Income

Take Your Passion for Writing and Build It into a Profitable Business

WRITE YOUR WAY TO A 6-FIGURE INCOME: TAKE YOUR PASSION FOR WRITING AND BUILD IT INTO A PROFITABLE BUSINESS

First edition. October 1, 2023.

Written by Matt Weik.

Introduction

Welcome to "Write Your Way to a 6-Figure Income." In this opening chapter, we embark on a journey together into the world of writing and the remarkable opportunities it offers in today's economy.

As the author of this book, I am excited to share my knowledge and insights, but before we dive into the wealth of information that lies ahead, let's take a moment to set the stage, explore the power of writing, and understand what this book has in store for you.

Welcome and Author's Credentials

First and foremost, I want to extend a warm welcome to you, the reader, for choosing this book as your guide on your path to a six-figure income through writing. Whether you're an aspiring writer, a seasoned wordsmith looking to expand your horizons, or someone simply curious about the possibilities, I'm delighted to have you on this journey.

Allow me to introduce myself briefly. My name is Matt Weik, and I've spent 20+ years in the world of writing, during which I've had the privilege of writing for over 100 magazines, been featured on 15,000+ websites with my content, and have published more than a dozen books.

Presently, I own and operate two writing businesses — Weik Fitness and Writing Rebels. Feel free to check them out below:

www.WeikFitness.com

www.TheWritingRebels.com

In addition to my writing businesses, I'm also an investor in several companies outside the writing world.

My passion for writing has not only been a source of personal fulfillment but has also allowed me to achieve financial success beyond my wildest expectations. I'm excited to share the insights, strategies, and lessons I've learned along the way to help you reach similar heights in your writing career.

The Power of Writing in Today's Economy

In the digital age, the written word has taken on new significance and power. Writing is no longer confined to the realms of books and newspapers — it has become a fundamental currency of communication in today's economy. In this section, we explore the transformative role of writing in the modern world.

We begin by discussing how the internet and digital technology have democratized the field of writing. With the rise of blogs, social media, eBooks, and online content, the barriers to entry have lowered, allowing individuals from all walks of life to become writers and reach global audiences.

The prevalence of written content across various platforms, from websites and social media to email marketing and e-commerce, has created an insatiable demand for skilled writers. We will explore how businesses, organizations, and individuals leverage the power of writing to connect with their audiences, drive engagement, and achieve their goals.

Writing is not only a means of communication but also a valuable asset. We discuss how quality content can establish authority, build trust, and drive results in diverse fields, from marketing and branding to education and thought leadership. Writing can be a powerful tool for personal and professional growth when done effectively.

What to Expect from This Book

Now that you have a glimpse of the transformative power of writing in today's economy, let's set the stage for what lies ahead in this book.

In the chapters to come, we will embark on a comprehensive exploration of the writing landscape, from understanding the writing industry's current state to uncovering the myriad of opportunities available to writers today. We will dive deeper into the mindset required for success, the development of essential writing skills, and the art of choosing the right niche.

You can look forward to practical guidance on setting up your writing business, creating a winning portfolio, navigating freelancing and content platforms, pitching to clients and publications, leveraging your network, and something everyone should be striving for... building passive income streams.

Financial aspects are not forgotten as we explore budgeting, taxes, saving, and investing strategies tailored to the unique needs of freelance writers. We will also delve into the art of building your personal brand and honing your time management and productivity skills.

Ultimately, this book is designed to be a comprehensive roadmap for writers of all levels and backgrounds who aspire to turn their passion for writing into a lucrative career.

Whether you're dreaming of a six-figure income, seeking to enhance your writing skills, or simply curious about the writing profession, there is valuable knowledge and inspiration awaiting you in these pages.

With all that being said, I'm not writing this book as some "secret sauce" or some shortcut to earning six figures. Nothing works unless you do, and if you implement the things discussed in this book, you will be on your way to exponentially increase your income through writing.

While there are some strategies within these pages that can provide you with an advantage over many writers, the fact still remains that you're going to need to consistently be working on all the skills and strategies I laid out. This will not come overnight. But over time, you will see incredible growth in your income from this skill.

As you begin your journey through the world of writing, keep an open mind, a pen at the ready, and your aspirations high. Together, we'll explore the vast landscape of writing opportunities and equip you with the tools, knowledge, and mindset to write your way to a six-figure income and beyond. If you're ready, let's begin this exciting adventure together.

Part I: Preparing for Success

Chapter 1
Understanding the Landscape

The journey to a six-figure income as a writer begins with a deep understanding of the landscape in which you operate. This chapter serves as the foundation for your writing career, providing valuable insights into the state of the writing industry, the diverse opportunities that exist today, and the need to dispel common myths and misconceptions.

The State of the Writing Industry

The writing industry has undergone a profound transformation in recent years, shaped by the digital revolution and the ever-evolving needs of businesses and readers alike. Understanding the current state of the industry is essential as it forms the backdrop against which your writing career will unfold.

First, we explore the impact of the digital age on the writing industry. The advent of the internet has democratized access to information and created an insatiable demand for written content. Businesses, websites, blogs, social media, and eBooks all rely on written words to communicate their messages, products, and ideas to a global audience. This digital shift has not only expanded the scope of writing opportunities but has also altered the way writers work, collaborate, and deliver content.

Moreover, we delve into the pervasive role of content in the modern world. Content has become a currency of communication, and writers are the architects of this new language. Whether it's crafting compelling blog posts, creating persuasive marketing copy, or engaging readers through storytelling, the writing industry is deeply embedded in various sectors, making skilled writers indispensable.

We also explore the emerging trends in content consumption. Video scripts, social media posts, email marketing campaigns, and interactive web content are just a few examples of how content has diversified. As a writer, adapting to these changing formats and platforms can open doors to exciting opportunities.

As I like to tell people... WORDS HAVE POWER.

The power of words can transform a business, drive traffic to a website, improve sales conversions, and build trust and authority among your followers, community, and peers.

The Freelance Boom

The freelance writing sector, once considered a niche pursuit, has blossomed into a thriving industry in its own right. As you start your journey to a six-figure writing income, it's essential to recognize the significance of freelancing in today's writing landscape.

Freelancers now constitute a substantial portion of the writing workforce, and we'll look at the factors contributing to this rise. This includes the allure of flexibility, the diversity of projects, and the potential for a lucrative income that comes with freelancing.

Today, more people than ever are working from home. Remote work has now become commonplace for many businesses, which has also opened the idea of not having in-house writers or marketing teams. As businesses begin finding the value in not having to pay salaries, benefits, and having large offices and headquarters, it has opened the door for freelancers to fill the gaps and needs.

However, we'll still address the realities of freelancing, including the competitive nature of the field, pricing pressures, and the need for self-discipline. Understanding these challenges is critical as you navigate the freelance landscape and decide whether or not jumping into this with both feet is for you.

Opportunities in Writing Today

The opportunities for writers today are as diverse as the craft itself. In this section, we unveil the multitude of paths you can take to craft a successful writing career, each offering its unique rewards and challenges.

Traditional writing careers, such as journalism, continue to thrive, both in print and digital formats. Journalists in the modern age include investigative reporting, feature writing, and digital journalism.

Copywriting, another traditional field, plays a pivotal role in advertising and marketing. Copywriters create persuasive content that drives sales, shapes brand identities, and engages audiences across various media.

Technical writing, often overlooked but indispensable, involves translating complex information into user-friendly documentation. Technical writers in industries like technology, healthcare, and engineering help bridge the gap between experts and end-users.

In the realm of online writing opportunities, content creation is a vast domain. Writers contribute to the web by crafting blog posts, articles, web content, and other forms of digital content. Additionally, once a niche pursuit, blogging has become a legitimate career option, with opportunities for monetization and niche-specific success.

The self-publishing revolution has empowered writers to publish their own work in eBook formats and beyond. Self-publishing (such as the book you're reading) has reshaped the publishing landscape and how writers can profit from their creative endeavors.

Specialized writing niches, from health and wellness to finance and business, offer writers opportunities to dive deep into particular fields. There is the potential for writing about health, fitness, and wellness (all things I've been known for over the past 20+ years), including medical writing and content creation for health-related businesses. In the financial and business sectors, financial blogging, reports, and corporate communications are prime domains.

Writing in specialized fields like technology, software, and scientific research also presents rewarding paths for writers seeking niche expertise.

Overcoming Common Myths and Misconceptions

Before you take a leap of faith into your journey toward a six-figure writing income, it's essential to dispel some common myths and misconceptions that can hinder your progress.

Myth #1: Writers Can't Earn a Decent Income

For some reason, there is the belief that writing is a low-paying profession. I can tell you from first-hand experience that writing can easily produce a six-figure income with the right strategies and mindset in place.

Myth #2: Writing is Easy and Anyone Can Do It

This simply is not true. There are plenty of people who put in the time to become a better writer and never become one. It's an art and a craft. Sure, you could take classes and practice, yet still never become anywhere close to the level of a professional writer. Writing is a skill that requires dedication and practice. You will need to continuously look to improve your skills and the value of honing your craft.

Myth #3: You Need a Degree in Writing to Succeed

While formal education can be beneficial, talent, experience, and a strong portfolio often matter more than a degree. For example, I have a degree in Kinesiology and Business from Penn State. I never took formal writing classes, it's just something that always came naturally to me. I've spent a lot of time reading books and watching videos on how to improve my skills and craft. You don't need a fancy degree in writing to earn a six-figure income.

Myth #4: Writing is a Solitary Pursuit

While you could certainly work alone as a writer, in today's collaborative world, writers often work in teams and collaborate with editors, designers, and marketers. Many times, networking and building relationships are the most important assets you have as a writer.

Myth #5: You Must Write Bestsellers to Succeed

Success in writing doesn't always require a New York Times bestseller. I've never made such a list, and my monthly passive income from my books is quite impressive. Additionally, you don't even need to write a book to make a six-figure income as a writer. If you create content and copy for brands and build your portfolio, you could create a very lucrative writing business for yourself.

CHAPTER 1 SUMMARY AND KEY TAKEAWAYS

- The digital age has transformed the writing industry, creating a high demand for written content across various platforms.
- Content has become a crucial currency of communication, making skilled writers indispensable.
- Adaptation to changing content formats and platforms is essential for writers to seize exciting opportunities.
- Freelance writing has become a thriving industry due to its flexibility, project diversity, and income potential.
- Remote work has made businesses more open to hiring freelancers over in-house teams.
- Freelancing comes with challenges like competition, pricing pressures, and the need for self-discipline.
- Various writing career paths exist, including journalism (print and digital), copywriting (advertising and marketing), technical writing (user-friendly documentation), and content creation (web content, blogging).
- Self-publishing empowers writers to profit from their creative work.
- Specialized writing niches like health, finance, technology, and more offer lucrative opportunities for niche expertise.

Chapter 2
Building the Writer's Mindset

In the journey to a six-figure income as a writer, the right mindset is your compass, guiding you through the challenges and triumphs of your career. This chapter explores the crucial elements of cultivating a growth mindset, dealing with self-doubt and imposter syndrome, and setting realistic expectations for yourself as a writer.

Cultivating a Writer's Mindset Towards Growth

A growth mindset is the belief that abilities and intelligence can be developed through dedication and hard work. It is the cornerstone of a successful writing career, enabling you to embrace challenges, learn from failures, and continually improve your skills.

First, we need to dive into and understand the concept of a growth mindset versus a fixed mindset.

A fixed mindset assumes that talent and abilities are innate and unchangeable, leading to a fear of failure and a reluctance to take risks.

In contrast, a growth mindset thrives on challenges, viewing failures as opportunities for growth and setbacks as stepping stones toward success. As a writer, adopting a growth mindset is essential for overcoming obstacles and realizing your full potential.

The power of belief is a central theme in cultivating a growth mindset. If you believe that you can develop your skills and achieve your goals through effort and dedication, you are more likely to persist in the face of difficulties. This belief in your capacity for growth fuels your motivation and resilience as a writer.

Embracing challenges is another aspect of a growth mindset. We discuss the importance of reframing setbacks as opportunities for learning and growth. Rather than viewing writer's block or rejection as insurmountable barriers, writers with a growth mindset see them as challenges to be overcome. This perspective shift empowers you to persevere through the inevitable ups and downs of a writing career.

There will be times when work from clients is slow (the seasonality of various industries). But that doesn't mean you should sit back with your feet up. You can always be working towards building out your portfolio and website with your own content to draw eyeballs to your work as well as you as a writer.

Your goal should be to showcase your work and get people interested in working with you. It's the ABCs of a successful business (Always Be Closing).

Dealing with Self-Doubt and Imposter Syndrome

One of the greatest challenges writers face is the battle with self-doubt and imposter syndrome. These internal struggles can hinder progress, stifle creativity, and erode self-confidence. In this section, we'll address these issues head-on and provide strategies to overcome them.

First, we define imposter syndrome — a phenomenon where individuals doubt their abilities and fear being exposed as frauds despite evidence of their competence. Recognizing imposter syndrome is the first step in conquering it. We explore common triggers, such as receiving praise or taking on new challenges, and the impacts of imposter syndrome on your writing career, including self-sabotage and missed opportunities.

I've dealt with this in my own career simply because I didn't think I was good enough at what I did, despite the knowledge to put into my content. Not having a degree in journalism made me feel like people would judge my grammar, etc., and that people wouldn't want to read my content.

While I put in the work to learn more about writing through reading books and YouTube videos from professional writers and authors, I also leveraged the power of software, such as Grammarly. Even though I go through to edit and check my work, there are always things I may miss or overlook. Grammarly is great at catching these for me (and best of all, they have a free version so that you don't even need to spend a dime on using it).

The key is to understand that no one is perfect. It takes authors years to publish a bestselling novel. They comb through their work methodically and intensely and scrutinize it until it basically drives them mad. But that goes back to what was said in the previous section, where writers need to focus on the growth mindset — the willingness to continually improve.

Strategies to overcome imposter syndrome are a critical focus of this section. Self-reflection techniques are invaluable for identifying and challenging negative self-talk. It's important to acknowledge your achievements, no matter how small, and reframe self-doubt into affirmations of your competence.

Setting realistic goals is another key strategy. By breaking down your writing goals into achievable steps, you can build confidence and track your progress. You need to set achievable goals that align with your current skill level while stretching your abilities to foster growth — always look to improve. Writers who are complacent very rarely will ever see a six-figure income from their work because they don't possess the will to want to work hard enough to achieve such an accomplishment.

Seeking support is also crucial in the battle against imposter syndrome. You should surround yourself with a support system, which may include mentors, peers, and writing communities. These individuals can provide guidance, perspective, and encouragement when self-doubt creeps in. Lean on them when you need to and provide the same back to them in return.

Finally, you need to understand the significance of celebrating your achievements. Acknowledging your successes, no matter how small, reinforces your self-esteem and counteracts the negative effects of imposter syndrome. By recognizing your accomplishments and attributing them to your efforts and skills, you can build a strong foundation of self-confidence.

As with any business, you want to stack your wins. Don't achieve one and then sit there celebrating while everyone around you is getting back to work. Sure, go ahead and celebrate (briefly), but you can't allow complacency to seep in. The great Babe Ruth was quoted saying, "Yesterday's home runs don't win today's games." Enjoy the moment of the win, but tomorrow is another day for you to get after it.

Setting Realistic Expectations

Managing expectations is a critical aspect of a successful writing career. In this section, we'll discuss the importance of setting realistic goals and expectations to navigate the highs and lows of the profession.

One thing you need to understand is the pitfalls that come along with setting unrealistic expectations, including the risks of expecting overnight success and setting the bar too high. Writers who anticipate immediate fame and fortune often encounter frustration and disappointment. We emphasize the importance of patience and persistence in achieving long-term success.

Some writers publish content on their websites and expect their traffic to soar, but it never happens. I should be preaching to the choir here, but building out content and SEO is a long game. You'll never find overnight success with anything in life. While to others, it may look like it, they don't see the long nights and tireless work you've put into building the momentum for it to look like an "overnight success."

Something else to watch out for is the comparison trap. This is a very common pitfall many writers will find themselves in. Comparing yourself to other writers can lead to feelings of inadequacy and dissatisfaction. We discuss strategies for focusing on your unique journey and growth rather than measuring your success against others.

Many will say I'm cocky for thinking this way, but I don't feel like I have competitors. I recommend everyone think this way. People often ask me who my competitors are in the health, fitness, nutrition, and supplement niche, and I tell them I don't have any. Why? Because I know the content I'm putting out is my best work. It doesn't matter what other writers out there are doing. All I can control is me and my work, so why should I focus on or worry about what others are doing? Let them think about me. The more focus I put into "competitors," the less focus and time I can put into my work.

Next is a topic many writers run into quite often. Luckily, I feel like with my mindset and drive, I've been able to avoid this during my 20+ year career as a writer. What is it? Burnout. Burnout is a significant concern in a profession that often demands long hours and intensive mental effort. You need to understand the dangers of overworking to meet unrealistic goals and explore the importance of work-life balance and self-care. If you feel you're burning yourself out or suffering from "writer's block," you need to take a step away, go have some fun away from writing, and then come back after you feel refreshed and energized.

I will say this just to put things into perspective. I write anywhere from 8-16 hours a day. On any given day, I can create upwards of 6-8 quality pieces of content for clients or my own website. Many look at that as insanity, banging away at a keyboard all those hours. For me, I love it. I get excited each morning when I wake up to go to the office and start writing. But you also need to realize that we are different people. You may be able to put in a few hours and then need to take a long break to regain your focus and mental energy. The key is to do what you need to in order to put out the best content possible.

Developing a realistic writing plan is a fundamental strategy for setting achievable goals. I like to use the SMART (Specific, Measurable, Achievable, Relevant, Time-Bound) framework for goal setting. This framework helps you define clear and actionable objectives, track your progress, and adapt your goals as needed.

Remember, you don't know what you don't know, so if you aren't tracking things, you'll never know where you were, are currently, or if you're on track with your goals. Therefore, creating a SMART system is important for your overall success.

We also need to emphasize the importance of creating a writing schedule that aligns with your life and priorities. A realistic and sustainable routine can prevent burnout and help you make steady progress toward your goals.

Using myself as an example. I'm a father to three boys and a husband to my wife. On top of those daily responsibilities, I make time in my schedule to hit a workout, do a red-light therapy session, get in a grounding session, sweat it out in my sauna, coach all the baseball teams my boys play on, and still find some time at night to unwind with a book or content that helps improve my skills (I'm a huge believer in you should always be learning).

How do I fit all of that in on top of all the hours of writing? I prioritize things and schedule them in my calendar. Things that go into the calendar are all priorities to me, and I refuse to allow anything to knock me off my schedule.

Measuring progress and adjusting your goals is the final component of setting realistic expectations. You must track your achievements, learn from setbacks, and stay focused on your long-term vision. By consistently evaluating your progress and adapting your goals, you can maintain motivation and continue advancing your writing career.

But none of that can be done if you aren't writing things down and tracking your progress. Be methodical and almost obsessive with it. Data and numbers don't like. So, stop thinking things are going well if you don't know. Utilizing data and numbers will give you an accurate representation of how close you are to hitting your goals.

CHAPTER 2 SUMMARY AND KEY TAKEAWAYS

- A growth mindset, believing that skills can be developed through hard work, is crucial for a successful writing career.
- It contrasts with a fixed mindset that assumes abilities are innate and unchangeable, leading to a fear of failure.
- Embracing challenges and viewing setbacks as opportunities for learning and growth is key to a growth mindset.
- Imposter syndrome involves doubting abilities despite evidence of competence and can hinder progress and creativity.
- Strategies to overcome imposter syndrome include self-reflection, setting achievable goals, seeking support, and celebrating achievements.
- Setting unrealistic expectations can lead to frustration and disappointment in a writing career.
- Pitfalls include expecting overnight success, falling into the comparison trap, and experiencing burnout.
- Strategies for setting realistic expectations include using the SMART goal framework, creating a sustainable writing schedule, and measuring progress to adapt goals accordingly. Tracking data is crucial for accurate goal assessment.

Chapter 3
Developing Your Writing Skills

In this chapter, we will dive into the foundational aspects of enhancing your writing skills. Writing, much like any other craft, is an art that thrives on continuous improvement and refinement. Whether you're a seasoned writer or just getting started, the path to mastery is paved with dedication to learning and growth.

The Importance of Continuous Learning

Writing is a dynamic skill that evolves over time, making it essential to adopt a mindset of perpetual learning. Successful writers understand that the journey to excellence is ongoing and that stagnation is the enemy of progress.

Reading Widely

Reading serves as a cornerstone of a writer's education. It's not merely about perusing texts but also about delving into a diverse range of genres, styles, and formats. By exploring different literary landscapes, writers can expand their horizons and infuse fresh elements into their work. Diving into varied genres allows you to draw inspiration and enrich your writing with new perspectives and storytelling techniques.

Moreover, analyzing the writing styles of accomplished authors can be a powerful learning tool. When you critically examine their work, you gain invaluable insights into the craft. You can dissect their storytelling methods, character and tone development, and narrative structures to understand what makes their writing compelling.

Writing Regularly

The best way to become a better writer is simply by writing more. Whenever you have free time, start writing and then analyze what you produced. Learn from your mistakes and understand the things you did differently from previous content so that you can continue to compound the skills you learn and practice.

Writing regularly is key to forging a path toward mastery. It's about cultivating the writing habit — a practice that's fundamental to honing your skills. A consistent writing routine not only sharpens your abilities but also fosters discipline and creativity. Establishing a dedicated writing schedule, whether it's daily, weekly, or tailored to your own rhythm, provides a framework for improvement.

Journaling is another powerful tool in your arsenal. It offers a safe space for experimentation and self-reflection. Through journaling, you can explore new ideas, refine your voice, and gain a deeper understanding of your own thoughts and emotions. This practice serves as a wellspring of creativity and personal growth, nurturing your writing skills in profound ways.

Improving Grammar and Style

Grammar and style are the foundational pillars of effective writing. They underpin your ability to convey ideas clearly and engage your readers. This section dives into techniques for refining your grammar and crafting a distinctive writing style that sets you apart from all the other writers in the niche you choose to be a part of.

Grammar Mastery

A solid grasp of grammar rules is non-negotiable for any writer. It forms the bedrock of your writing, ensuring that your prose is clear and free from distracting errors. This includes understanding sentence structure, punctuation conventions, and common pitfalls that writers often encounter. Effective writing is rooted in precision, and grammar is the compass that guides you.

Furthermore, the art of editing and proofreading should never be underestimated. Meticulous attention to detail is what separates good writing from exceptional writing. It's the painstaking process of reviewing and refining your work to ensure it's polished and error-free. Grammar resources like grammar books, websites, and tools like Grammarly can be your trusty writing companions. They offer guidance and reference points to help you fine-tune your writing.

Crafting Your Style

Crafting a unique writing style is the hallmark of a distinguished writer. It's about finding and nurturing your distinctive voice — a voice that resonates with your readers and sets your work apart. Developing your style is an exploration of self-expression and creativity.

Your style isn't merely about how you write, it's also about what you write. Understanding tone and audience is pivotal. Different genres and audiences demand different writing styles. Whether you're crafting a lighthearted blog post or a formal research paper, adapting your style to suit the context and expectations of your audience is essential.

Moreover, the art of simplicity is a treasure in writing. Clarity and conciseness make your writing more accessible and engaging. In a world inundated with information, readers appreciate writing that communicates effectively without unnecessary complexity. Techniques for achieving this balance will be explored in this section, helping you refine your style into one that captivates and resonates.

Oftentimes, I have people contact me and ask if I can write content for their blog or website. They mention that they like the way I write and that whenever they read an article, they can immediately tell if I wrote it or not (if you read blogs of various supplement brand websites, there is an extremely high probability that I wrote the article, even if no author credit is given).

I often wondered what they meant when they said such things. What makes my writing so different that the reader can pick things out of it and give it away that I'm the author of the piece? I finally asked a prospect who called me up one day, and they told me that I have a way with words that pulls people in while providing insane amounts of knowledge and value to the reader and that my ability to sometimes add humor into the fold is almost always a dead giveaway.

What does this mean for you? It means that you need to have your own personality when writing. Sure, you can take things from writers you respect and enjoy, but you need to be able to craft your content in a way that it creates and follows your writing persona to help set you apart from everyone else who writes similar content.

Research and Fact-Checking Techniques

Inaccuracies can significantly diminish your credibility as a writer, whether you're crafting fiction or non-fiction. This section will equip you with the essential skills of effective research and meticulous fact-checking.

Conducting Effective Research

Research forms the backbone of informative and authoritative writing. It's about gathering information, evidence, and insights to support your narrative, argument, or topic you're trying to help the reader better understand.

Here are some key components of conducting effective research:

Choosing Reliable Sources

The credibility of your writing hinges on the reliability of your sources. Selecting reputable sources, whether you're conducting research for a novel or a non-fiction piece, is incredibly important as you want to provide the reader with factual information from a reputable source instead of someone who is just throwing around their opinion with nothing to back up their claims. Knowing where to find trustworthy information is a crucial skill for any writer. PubMed is one of the best places to start if you're adding factual research to any piece of content you write.

Organizing Information

As you delve into your research, the sheer volume of information can be overwhelming. Techniques for efficiently collecting, categorizing, and organizing research materials will help you maintain clarity and focus. An organized approach ensures that you can readily access and reference your sources as needed.

Avoiding Plagiarism

This should go without saying, but ethical writing involves giving proper credit to your sources and avoiding plagiarism. It's vital that you cite your references, strategize for paraphrasing, and quote effectively. Upholding academic and ethical standards in your writing is paramount. If you get caught stealing other people's work by plagiarizing and calling it your own, it will be difficult to win back your readers and followers, and your trust and authority in your industry may be destroyed.

Rigorous Fact-Checking

Fact-checking is the process of verifying the accuracy of information presented in your writing. Whether you're crafting a news article, a historical account, or even a work of fiction, maintaining factual integrity is essential.

Here are some things to consider:

Verifying Information

You need to create your own procedures for cross-referencing and fact-checking. This involves corroborating facts, figures, and details from multiple reliable sources. Verifying information ensures that your writing is accurate and free from inaccuracies.

Interviewing Experts

When writing about specialized topics, interviewing experts can provide invaluable insights and primary sources of information. Consider conducting effective interviews by preparing thoughtful questions and extracting expert knowledge to enhance your writing.

Ethical Considerations

As a writer, you bear the ethical responsibility of presenting factual information. You need to maintain ethical considerations surrounding factual accuracy, transparency, and responsible reporting. Upholding ethical standards ensures that your readers can trust your work.

CHAPTER 3 SUMMARY AND KEY TAKEAWAYS

- Writing is a dynamic skill that requires continuous improvement and learning.
- Reading widely, analyzing accomplished authors' styles, and writing regularly are fundamental practices for writers to enhance their skills.
- A solid grasp of grammar rules and meticulous editing and proofreading are essential for effective writing.
- Crafting a unique writing style, adapting to different genres and audiences, and emphasizing simplicity and clarity are crucial aspects of a writer's style development.
- Developing your own writing persona and personality sets you apart from other writers in your niche.
- Effective research involves choosing reliable sources, organizing information efficiently, and avoiding plagiarism.
- Rigorous fact-checking involves verifying information, interviewing experts for specialized topics, and upholding ethical considerations for factual accuracy and responsible reporting.

Part II: Building Your Writing Career

Chapter 4
How I Stumbled Upon and Started My Writing Career

Everyone has a backstory. For me, it all led up to where I am today in my writing career. In this chapter, I want to run through my background to give you a better idea of how things seemingly fell into place with my writing career.

While I don't assume you will follow the same storyline nor have the same opportunities fall on your lap, we all need to understand our unique background and how it led us to what we're doing today and the professions we choose.

I have always had a passion for writing, but I want to run down exactly how things transpired before starting my own businesses in my 30s. By following my passions, with each passing year, things seemed to fall into place like a puzzle you don't have an image to help guide you, but as you keep working on it, the pieces simply seem to snap together until it's completed and you're left in awe, standing there looking at what you created.

No Keyboard Was Safe Around Me

As odd as it may sound, unbeknownst to me, my writing career started way back in elementary school. It took a while for me to understand my gift, and I really never wrapped my head around it until I was in college.

I was the oddball in the classroom who, throughout my years in school and college, preferred to write essays instead of taking multiple-choice and true-or-false tests. I would get nervous and anxious when taking such tests and always found myself second-guessing my answers.

On the other hand, if you gave me a blank piece of paper and told me to write about a topic, I could write and write until my pencil ran out of lead. For some reason, I was given the ability to write at a very young age, and I thoroughly enjoyed it.

When I was young (before computers were invented), my parents bought me an electronic typewriter. Depending on your age, you may not even know what that is. After a few years, we upgraded to an electronic word processor, which was like a glorified electronic typewriter. (I seem to really be dating myself and showing my age.)

Fast-forward a few more years, and I became a teenager, we upgraded to the Mack Daddy of them all, the Commodore 64. It was one of the first computers ever created, and while it was introduced the same year I was born (1982), it was extremely expensive for its time, and not many families had them in their homes just yet. While the Commodore 64 was massive, I was in awe and found myself on there, tapping away at the keyboard like it was my job. It was almost like I was foreshadowing my future now that I look back at it.

Helping Others Gave Me the Opportunity of a Lifetime

While in college, where I was studying Kinesiology and Business, I began engaging with other people on the Bodybuilding.com forums. At the time, Ryan Deluca had just started the website, and it was exploding in the fitness and bodybuilding industry. On the forums, I was answering questions with detailed answers to help people reach their health and fitness goals, taking the knowledge I built through reading books, magazines, and the information from my college courses.

One day, out of the blue, I got a message from Ryan asking me if I was interested in writing some articles for the website. He mentioned that he appreciated my knowledge and help on the forums and thought some additional content on the site would benefit his customers. I was one of the first writers to publish content on his website.

What began as one article per month turned into multiple per month. I then did contest coverage on top of my monthly articles to further grow their blossoming content. This is all where my writing career exploded. Today, Bodybuilding.com remains one of the largest health, fitness, and bodybuilding websites on the planet, with organic monthly traffic of nearly 11 million users. I am honored to have been one of the writing pioneers in the industry.

Doors Were Opening All Over the Place

After several months of writing content for Bodybuilding.com in college, I had a few fitness and bodybuilding magazines reach out to me, inquiring if I'd be interested in writing for their publications. I accepted, and that's really where the gasoline was tossed into the fire. My writing career was a raging inferno, with offers coming in from all over. I was not only writing for magazines and websites in the United States but also for magazines overseas.

Writing wasn't my only passion at the time. While in college, I became a certified personal trainer, strength coach, and sports nutritionist. I began working with clients at a local gym and was hired as a local high school's strength and conditioning coach. I continued this even after earning my diploma from Penn State in Kinesiology and Business. I thought I was living on cloud nine, and things couldn't get any better for me.

Then, out of the blue, another door opened. As I was on the bodybuilding.com forums, I received a message from someone who worked at MET-Rx — one of the biggest supplement brands in the world at the time. They offered me a position as a forum representative for the brand, where I would represent MET-Rx in the Bodybuilding.com forums and answer product-related questions. As a fan of MET-Rx and someone who used their products religiously, I accepted their offer.

As time passed, I continued training at the gyms and the local high school while also producing a ton of content for websites and magazines. Then, another door opened. MET-Rx just so happened to be looking for a regional manager in my area, and being that I already knew everything about the brand and products, they offered me the position. The national sales director flew up to the Philly Airport and met with me. Everything he said sounded great. The salary was much more than I was making training clients, I had the option of a fantastic retirement plan, I got a company car, daily per diem while traveling on the road for business — the list went on and on. I accepted and gave up training my clients and athletes.

With MET-Rx, I managed 12 states in the Mid-Atlantic region and handled a book of business worth several million dollars between distributors, supplement stores, and gyms. I traveled every week, and while in hotels every night, I passed the time in my hotel room by continuing to write for all the websites and publications I previously worked with. Being that MET-Rx knew I could write, I began writing their product pages, label copy, and other key pieces of copy for the brand.

Later in my career with MET-Rx, I was promoted to run their entire Team Sports division, where I would work with high schools, colleges, and professional sports teams to get our products into their hands for the athletes. Knowing the lingo and requirements needed for athletes to improve their recovery and performance, I was a natural fit.

Before I knew it, I was working with the biggest teams and athletes on the planet, and my name was getting out in the industry. I was even featured in several magazines, such as Money Magazine and Personal Trainer Magazine, for my work in the fitness and supplement industry. Who would have thought that my ugly mug would be on the cover of magazines?

Mind you, I'm still producing content for all the websites and print magazines this entire time. While I had a lot on my plate, I loved every minute.

After nearly a decade with MET-Rx, I sat down with the executives at MET-Rx to explain my plan and strategy for the next year and what I needed from them to continue growing the division triple digits every year. Unfortunately, their vision and my vision were not aligned. I was at a crossroads of sorts. Do I stay with MET-Rx or find something else? After a call with the executive team, we decided it was best if we parted ways. There were no hard feelings, and to this day, I wish them nothing but the best. But I knew exactly what my plan was next.

Forging My Way Through Passion

It was no secret that I loved writing. I could do it all day, every day, and never get sick of it. When I sat down with my wife and discussed my passion for leaving corporate America and forging my own path by starting my own business, I expected her to say I was utterly insane and needed to see a therapist because, at the time, we just had our first son. Instead, she said, "I know you'll make it happen — go for it." Within a week of my departure from MET-Rx, I had already filed my LLC and started building what would be my first fulfilling and profitable writing business.

In my first year of business, I had already surpassed the income I would have made at MET-Rx and was building the six-figure income I had always thought was destined for me. I knew I was on to something. That said, my success wouldn't have been possible if it weren't for the network I built during my time in the supplement industry and following I grew on the Bodybuilding.com forums.

As word got around that I was no longer with MET-Rx and I started my own writing business (Weik Fitness), brands came out of the woodwork and contacted me to help them build out their blog content and copy on their product pages.

You can say from there the rest is history. But I wasn't done or satisfied. I wanted to build something even bigger.

Taking a Boring Niche and Creating Something Fun and Unique

Most people in the writing services business are pretty dry, almost robotic. And I totally get it and understand why. I don't mean that in a mean way, but many people look at writing content as monotonous and boring. To some extent, I can completely see their point.

If you do not love to write, sitting down to write a blog article or copy for a product or product page could feel like wasted time. By the time you press that final period, you're probably left with something you don't like and feel you need to start over from scratch. There's where a content writer or copywriter like me comes riding in like a white knight to save the day.

The typical conversation between a brand and wordsmith tends to be very straightforward: a strict business relationship, no fluff, no fun, just transactional. Me, I hate that. I like to have fun in everything I do, and I want the people I work with to look at me as a friend and someone they can joke around with and enjoy talking with.

Part of the reason I left corporate America is because I'm not the most politically correct person on the planet. Those in the fitness and supplement industry know how I am, my humor, and they appreciate our relationship — both on a personal and professional level. I wanted to expand that experience with other industries that yawned every time they reached out to a writer.

That's where my second business was born — Writing Rebels.

Writing Rebels isn't your boring, stuffy writing company like you'll find while scouring the internet. And we have a guarantee to all our clients that we showcase on the homepage.

This guarantee reads as follows...

"Here at Writing Rebels, we like to have fun. Our professional writing services cater to companies, both big and small, as well as individuals who don't have the time or simply don't want to create some form of content or copy. Our motto is to produce the best product possible for our clients on time, all while enjoying the process. Let's be real, if you're like most people, you don't consider writing a pleasant experience (which is probably why you came to our website). You can count 2,593,278 better things to do than sit down and write. That's where we come in. We love to write! Maybe we're weird? (But in a good way)

Our clients are like friends (and no, not your typical "work friends" like the guy in the office next to you who you keep ducking his lunch invite). We're the type of company that will provide you with unmatched service, and by the end of the project, you'll want to go grab a coffee. And if there's coffee involved, we're there! We guarantee that working with us will be unlike any other project you've outsourced in the past. At Writing Rebels, we take pride in knowing we've gone above and beyond to make this process simple, easy, and convenient. Are you ready to get started?"

We don't want to be the norm. In fact, we break the norm at Writing Rebels. It's exactly why the word "REBELS" is in our business name. We go against the grain but in a good way.

I'm not sharing this to toot my own horn or pitch you my services, it's to get the gears in your brain turning about your own future and ideas you may have.

The biggest hurdle you'll want to overcome when starting your writing business and turning it into a six-figure income is how you'll differentiate yourself from everyone else. That's precisely what I did with Writing Rebels. And in our first year of doing business, we generated over six figures. Don't be average, be extraordinary.

Now, let's help you figure out how you can find your own niche and start building your six-figure income through writing.

Chapter 5
Choosing Your Niche

In this pivotal chapter, we'll talk about the intricate process of selecting your writing niche, a defining aspect of your writing career that sets the course for your success. Your niche is more than just a topic, it's the domain where your passion and expertise converge to create a unique identity as a writer.

Identifying Your Passion and Expertise

Discovering your niche begins with introspection. It's about uncovering your passions, those subjects that truly ignite your creativity and enthusiasm. What topics make your heart race, and what issues do you find yourself deeply engaged with?

For me, I've always been passionate about health, fitness, workouts, nutrition, and supplements. I actually went to college for Kinesiology, and much of what I learned and took away from my courses helped me insert key elements in my content.

That said, I'm also heavily involved in the firearms and tactical world, working with many firearms instructors around the United States. I've been able to combine each of these industries into my content that gets thousands of views.

The goal was to take my passions and things I'm most knowledgeable in and create content around those topics to provide my readers and followers with valuable information they can implement in their lives.

Here are some of the seeds you need to consider and plant in your niche:

Self-Reflection: Take time to reflect on your interests, hobbies, and what truly excites you (after all, do you really want to write about things you don't enjoy for the rest of your life?). Think about the subjects you'd love to explore through writing, even if you weren't getting paid for it. Often, our passions provide essential clues about our ideal niche.

Exploring Hobbies and Interests: Your hobbies and personal interests can serve as fertile ground for niche selection. For instance, if you're an avid gardener, there's potential in writing about gardening tips, plant care, or sustainable landscaping. If you're into fitness like me, make that your niche. Simply leverage the things you enjoy and know the most about rather than topics or hobbies you don't know much about or don't enjoy. A lack of passion will show through in your content.

Your Personal Journey: Your unique life experiences can also shape your niche. Personal narratives and life lessons can be a rich source of content. Think about how your own journey can resonate with and inspire others. Being able to add personal experiences to your content will provide added value to your content that others may not be able to recreate.

Moving beyond passion, your expertise also plays a pivotal role in niche selection. Consider your professional background, education, and skills. What are you exceptionally knowledgeable about? Your expertise can form the bedrock of your niche, providing credibility and authority to your writing.

Professional Background: Your past or current profession might offer a treasure trove of niche possibilities. For example, if you have a background in healthcare, medical writing or health-related topics could be a natural fit. Using myself as an example, I am a personal trainer, strength coach, and sports nutritionist. To top that off, I worked for one of the largest supplement companies, where I ran one of their divisions for a decade. Therefore, I'm able to take my "expertise" and apply it to my writing.

Education and Training: Formal education can be a valuable asset in your niche selection. If you hold a degree or certification in a particular field, consider how it can be leveraged in your writing career. Going back to my educational background, having a Kinesiology and Business degree helped me with much of the knowledge for my content. That said, you don't need a degree in order to be a writer and build a six-figure income.

Skill Assessment: Take stock of your writing skills. Identify your strengths, whether it's storytelling, technical writing, or persuasive copywriting. Your skill set can guide your niche selection towards areas where you excel. If you're great at copywriting, focus on that. If you're great at creating content for websites or blogs, do that. You need to go back to the self-reflection part mentioned above and think about what you're good at and like to do.

Researching Profitable Writing Niches

While following your passion and expertise is crucial, it's equally important to assess your chosen niche's market demand and profitability. A profitable niche not only sustains your writing career but also offers financial rewards.

Here are some things to consider:

Market Research: Conduct thorough market research to gauge the demand for content in your chosen niche. Explore trends, audience size, and the competition. Analyze whether your niche is growing, stable, or in decline. Tools like keyword research can provide insights into what people are actively searching for (you can use something like Google Keyword Planner, Yoast SEO, or similar tool).

Competitive Landscape: Evaluate the level of competition within your chosen niche. A highly competitive niche may require a more unique angle or specialization to stand out. Conversely, a niche with less competition might present a growth opportunity.

Monetization Potential: Understanding how your niche can translate into income is essential. Consider the various revenue streams available to writers within your niche. Are there opportunities for content creation, book publishing, online courses, or consulting services? Assess the pricing strategies prevalent in your niche to ensure your rates are competitive.

Long-Term Viability: While immediate profits are enticing, it's wise to think long-term. Evaluate whether your niche has staying power. Some niches may be trendy but short-lived, while others provide consistent opportunities over time. Staying attuned to industry trends can help you anticipate shifts in demand.

Balancing Passion with Market Demand

The ideal niche strikes a balance between your passion and market demand. While writing about your passions can be deeply fulfilling, it's equally vital to consider whether there's an audience eager to consume content on those subjects.

Aligning Passion and Demand: The sweet spot lies in finding niches where your passion intersects with market demand. This intersection not only fuels your enthusiasm but also ensures there's an audience eager to engage with your work.

Flexibility: Flexibility within your niche is an asset. As your writing career evolves, you may discover new interests or areas of expertise. Being adaptable allows you to pivot and explore new niches or sub-niches as your interests evolve.

Setting Realistic Expectations: While pursuing your passion is important, it's crucial to set realistic expectations. Understand that not all niches grow at the same pace. Some may offer immediate opportunities, while others require patience and persistence. Diversifying your niche portfolio can help mitigate risks and ensure a more stable income.

CHAPTER 5 SUMMARY AND KEY TAKEAWAYS

- Your niche should be based on your passions and interests, as well as your expertise and knowledge.
- Self-reflection, exploring hobbies and interests, and drawing from your personal journey can help identify your niche.
- Professional background, education, and skills also play a significant role in niche selection.
- Assess market demand and profitability in your chosen niche through thorough research.
- Evaluate the competitive landscape to determine how you can stand out.
- Consider different monetization potential within your niche and its long-term viability.
- The ideal niche balances your passion with market demand, ensuring there's an audience for your content.
- Flexibility within your niche allows you to adapt and explore new areas of interest.
- Set realistic expectations, as not all niches grow at the same pace, and diversify your niche portfolio for stability.

Chapter 6
Setting Up Your Writing Business

Moving along on your journey toward a six-figure income as a writer, it's crucial to establish a solid foundation for your writing business. This chapter will guide you through the essential steps of setting up your writing business, ensuring that you operate efficiently, professionally, and with a strong brand presence.

Legal Considerations and Business Structures

Before you dive headfirst into your writing career, it's vital to address the legal aspects and determine the most suitable business structure for your endeavor.

Understanding the legal considerations surrounding your writing business is crucial. This includes registering your business, obtaining any necessary permits or licenses, and complying with tax regulations. Depending on your location and the scale of your business, you may need to fulfill specific legal requirements.

Choosing the proper business structure is equally important. Common options for writers include sole proprietorship, limited liability company (LLC), or corporation. Each structure has its advantages and drawbacks in terms of liability, taxation, and administrative requirements. I encourage you to do some research on which would be ideal for your situation and circumstances.

Personally, being that I'm a "solopreneur" and have no partners or members of my business that have any say in my business, I choose to go the route of an LLC. I like that it provides protection should anything happen, such as a lawsuit against you or legal action be taken against your business. An LLC protects your personal assets from being taken in such instances and allows a clear separation between business and personal assets.

But again, you have to determine your risk level and then form your business however you deem appropriate. If it's going to be you and another individual, a partnership or corporation may be your best option. Something I would recommend you avoid is a sole proprietorship. Sure, it's the easiest to set up, but you don't get any protection like you would through something like an LLC or corporation.

Branding Yourself as a Writer

Your brand is your unique identity as a writer, and it plays a pivotal role in attracting clients and readers. Crafting a strong and memorable brand is essential for success in the writing industry.

When starting the process of defining your writer's brand, begin with a deep exploration of your writing style, voice, and values. Understanding your unique selling points and what sets you apart from other writers will serve as the foundation of your brand identity.

Once you've defined your brand, you need to understand the strategies you want to use to effectively communicate it to your target audience. This includes crafting a compelling author bio, designing a professional website, and creating a consistent brand voice across all your marketing materials (such as social media).

Don't overlook social media. Some people despise it, but it's free advertising when you think about it and a free way to get your content out in front of millions of eyeballs without having to pay for ads.

Furthermore, don't neglect the power of storytelling in branding. Sharing your personal journey, experiences, and passions can resonate with readers and clients, forging a deeper connection.

Building an Online Presence

In today's digital age, having a robust online presence is indispensable for writers. It's the gateway through which you can reach clients, readers, and collaborators. In this section, we'll guide you through the process of establishing and maintaining a compelling online presence.

Your website is a cornerstone of your online presence. You need a website —
this should be non-negotiable. There are several essential elements of a writer's
website, including creating a professional homepage, crafting an engaging
portfolio, and incorporating a blog to showcase your expertise and engage with
your audience.

Social media is a powerful tool for writers to connect with their audience and
expand their reach. You should absolutely leverage the various social media
platforms and how to strategically use them to build your brand and promote
your work. Utilize social platforms like LinkedIn, Facebook, Instagram,
Twitter, and Threads. If you're into video content, you can't forget platforms
like YouTube and TikTok.

Effective content marketing is another key component of your online presence.
You'll need to consider your content creation strategies, such as blogging, guest
posting, and email marketing, to help you establish yourself as an authority in
your niche and attract a loyal readership.

Additionally, think about the importance of online networking and engaging
with writing communities. Building relationships with fellow writers, clients,
and readers can open doors to opportunities and collaborations, further
enhancing your online presence. Joining groups on social media can do a great
job of connecting you with peers you should get to know, as well as groups that
are specific to your niche where you can share your content.

CHAPTER 6 SUMMARY AND KEY TAKEAWAYS

- Understand the legal requirements for your writing business, such as registration, permits, and tax compliance.
- Choose the proper business structure for your needs, considering options like sole proprietorship, LLC, or corporation.
- Protect your personal assets by opting for an LLC or corporation, which provides a clear separation between business and personal finances.
- Your writer's brand is your unique identity; define it based on your writing style, voice, and values.
- Communicate your brand effectively through strategies like author bios, professional websites, consistent brand voice, and storytelling.
- Utilize social media as a free advertising and content distribution tool to reach a broader audience.
- Create a professional author website with essential elements like a homepage, portfolio, and blog.
- Leverage social media platforms like LinkedIn, Facebook, Instagram, Twitter, YouTube, TikTok, and more to connect with your audience and promote your work.
- Implement content marketing strategies, such as blogging, guest posting, and email marketing, to establish authority in your niche.
- Engage with writing communities and online networks to build relationships with peers, clients, and readers, opening doors to opportunities and collaborations.

Chapter 7
Creating a Winning Portfolio

One of the most potent tools in your arsenal is a compelling portfolio when striving to build a successful writing career and attain a six-figure income. Your portfolio serves as a showcase of your skills, expertise, and the quality of your work. In this chapter, we will dive into the intricacies of creating a winning portfolio, a pivotal asset for attracting clients and opportunities in the competitive writing industry.

Selecting and Showcasing Your Best Work

The foundation of a powerful portfolio lies in the careful selection and presentation of your best work. Your portfolio is a reflection of your capabilities as a writer, making it imperative to curate a collection that demonstrates your proficiency and versatility.

To begin, consider the breadth and depth of your writing repertoire. Select a variety of pieces that highlight your skills across different genres, styles, and formats. This diversity not only showcases your adaptability but also appeals to a broader range of potential clients and readers.

Quality takes precedence over quantity in your portfolio. Handpick pieces that exemplify your finest craftsmanship and most engaging storytelling. Each piece should be a testament to your ability to captivate readers, convey ideas effectively, and meet the unique objectives of each project.

While assembling your portfolio, pay close attention to the organization and presentation. Clear and concise descriptions for each piece, outlining the context, objectives, and your role in the project, provide valuable context for prospective clients and readers. High-quality visuals, such as images, infographics, or links to published work, enhance the visual appeal and credibility of your portfolio.

Tailoring Your Portfolio to Your Niche

A well-crafted portfolio goes beyond showcasing your writing prowess, it also aligns with your chosen niche or areas of expertise. Tailoring your portfolio to a specific niche positions you as an authority in that field and increases your appeal to clients seeking specialized content.

Start by defining your niche. This could be a particular industry, such as technology, health, or finance, or a specific writing style, such as creative storytelling, technical documentation, or copywriting. Once you've identified your niche, strategically curate your portfolio to highlight your relevant work within that category.

For example, more than 20 years ago, I knew I wanted to write about health and fitness topics. From there, it branched out into nutrition and supplements as I expanded my credentials and became a certified sports nutritionist. The more my content was viewed, the more opportunities opened up for me. It started on Bodybuilding.com and then expanded out to various print magazines and other websites. Each time I published content, it was like a snowball effect where my authority got bigger and bigger in the industry.

Don't view your portfolio as you are "showing off." Your portfolio is like your business card. The more people you can put your portfolio in front of them, the more likely they are to want to work with you or, at a minimum, follow your work.

Consider the needs and expectations of clients in your niche. What type of content are they looking for? What are the key challenges or pain points they face? Your portfolio should not only showcase your ability to write within the niche but also address these specific client needs.

For instance, if you're targeting the healthcare industry, include pieces that demonstrate your knowledge of medical terminology, healthcare trends, and the ability to communicate complex medical information to a lay audience.

Furthermore, emphasize your niche expertise in the descriptions accompanying each portfolio item. Explain how your work in this particular niche has provided value, solved problems, or contributed to the success of previous clients. This positions you as a writer who not only understands the niche but also delivers tangible results.

Using Testimonials and Case Studies

Client testimonials and case studies serve as powerful endorsements of your skills and credibility as a writer. Incorporating these elements into your portfolio can significantly enhance its persuasive impact.

Testimonials are endorsements from clients or readers who have experienced your writing firsthand. These endorsements carry weight because they offer social proof of your abilities.

Reach out to satisfied clients and request permission to include their testimonials in your portfolio. Ensure that the testimonials are specific, highlighting the aspects of your writing that clients found most valuable.

Taking things a step further, case studies provide in-depth insights into your writing process and its impact on clients' objectives. A well-structured case study tells a compelling story of how you tackled a writing project, the challenges you overcame, and the positive outcomes you achieved. Include metrics, such as increased website traffic, higher engagement rates, or improved search engine rankings, to quantify the results.

When incorporating testimonials and case studies into your portfolio, strategically place them alongside the relevant portfolio items. For instance, if you have a case study showcasing your success in boosting a client's website traffic through SEO-optimized blog posts, include it next to the corresponding writing samples, such as the link to the particular piece of content or copy. This contextualizes the impact of your work and reinforces your value proposition.

CHAPTER 7 SUMMARY AND KEY TAKEAWAYS

- Curate your portfolio with care, focusing on quality over quantity.
- Include diverse pieces that demonstrate your proficiency across different genres, styles, and formats.
- Provide clear and concise descriptions for each portfolio item, outlining context, objectives, and your role.
- Enhance your portfolio with high-quality visuals, images, infographics, or links to published work.
- Define your niche or areas of expertise within the writing industry.
- Strategically curate your portfolio to highlight relevant work in your chosen niche.
- Consider client needs and expectations within the niche and address them in your portfolio.
- Emphasize your niche expertise in portfolio descriptions to showcase your understanding and results.
- Incorporate client testimonials that provide social proof of your writing abilities.
- Request specific testimonials that highlight the aspects of your writing that clients found most valuable.
- Create case studies to offer in-depth insights into your writing process and its impact on client objectives.
- Place testimonials and case studies strategically alongside relevant portfolio items to reinforce your value proposition.

Part III: Finding High-Paying Writing Gigs

Chapter 8
Freelancing and Content Platforms

In the world of freelance writing, tapping into the vast opportunities offered by content platforms is a key stepping stone to achieving a six-figure income. This chapter is dedicated to exploring the intricacies of freelancing and content platforms, providing insights into selecting the right platforms, navigating them effectively, and building a consistent income stream.

Platforms for Freelance Writers

The digital age has birthed a multitude of content platforms, each offering a unique ecosystem for freelance writers to thrive. However, not all platforms are created equal, and it's essential to choose wisely based on your goals, skills, and preferences.

To begin, we'll examine the diversity of content platforms available. Some platforms cater to a broad range of writing styles and niches, while others are niche-specific, focusing on particular industries or types of content. It's crucial to align your choice with your niche and writing expertise.

Understanding the different types of content platforms is equally important. These platforms can be broadly categorized into job boards, content marketplaces, and self-publishing platforms.

Job boards connect freelance writers with clients seeking specific writing services. Content marketplaces, on the other hand, allow writers to offer their services to a broader client base, often featuring a wide variety of content projects. Self-publishing platforms empower writers to publish their own work, whether it's eBooks, articles, or blog posts.

When just getting started, you may find it helpful to utilize websites like Fiverr and UpWork to pick up some writing gigs. While these can help bring in paying writing jobs, you'll want to build out a pipeline of potential clients you want to work with and reach out to them about your services.

Once you've identified your niche and the type of platform that suits your goals, we'll explore strategies for researching and evaluating specific platforms. This includes assessing factors like platform reputation, client base, payment terms, and competition. Thorough research and due diligence are essential in selecting platforms that align with your career objectives.

Strategies for Navigating Content Marketplaces

Content marketplaces are a prevalent choice for freelance writers looking to secure a steady flow of projects. However, these platforms are competitive environments, and navigating them effectively requires a strategic approach.

We'll begin by discussing the importance of crafting a compelling profile on content marketplaces. Your profile serves as your digital calling card, and it's essential to optimize it for maximum impact. You need to be very specific with your strategies for creating an attention-grabbing profile that highlights your expertise, experience, and writing style. Incorporating relevant keywords and showcasing a portfolio of your best work can significantly enhance your profile's visibility and attract potential clients.

Bidding on projects is a fundamental aspect of content marketplaces, and we'll explore strategies for crafting persuasive proposals. Effective proposals not only demonstrate your suitability for the project but also address the client's specific needs and objectives. We'll discuss techniques for tailoring your proposals to individual projects, showcasing your unique value proposition, and standing out among competing bids a little later.

Building long-term client relationships on content platforms is a valuable strategy for securing a steady income stream. Later, we'll discuss tactics for exceeding client expectations, delivering high-quality work consistently, and fostering trust and reliability.

The goal of these jobs is that you want to build a relationship with these businesses and brands so that they will continue hiring you for writing work. Repeat business and referrals from satisfied clients can be a significant source of income stability.

I will say this as I like to be fully transparent about my own writing businesses and how I built them. When it comes to websites like Fiverr and UpWork, many people have had great success with them. Personally, I found them to be a waste of time. Your mileage may vary, however. I found myself starting out trying to pick up some gigs here and there on the platforms, only to be spending way too much time writing proposal after proposal.

I pivoted away from these types of sites and focused on building my own website and then using my network (which I'll discuss later) to grow my business. Adding content to my website and optimizing it for SEO helped build my traffic. As more people and companies read my work, the more opportunities were presented to me.

If you were going to start out with Fiverr or UpWork, I still highly recommend you continue building out a website, which will also act as a gigantic portfolio of your work. I can't find a single negative that has come from building out my own websites and adding content to them.

Building a Steady Income Stream

Consistency is the bedrock of a successful freelance writing career, and building a steady income stream is a paramount goal. You may need to develop and implement strategies for achieving income stability through content platforms when you're first getting started (before completely building out your own website and funneling prospects through your contact page).

Diversification is a key principle for steady income. You should consider diversifying your client base, niches, and project types, as it can reduce income volatility. Pursuing a mix of short-term and long-term projects, as well as establishing retainer agreements with clients, can contribute to a more reliable income stream.

Building long-term relationships and working with brands will help prevent you from going months without seeing a paycheck. Knowing what you're making each month (or even getting some extra work on top of your typical projects) can help put your mind at ease so that you're not constantly worried and chasing your next paycheck.

Additionally, you will need to utilize time management strategies for balancing multiple projects effectively. Freelance writers often juggle several assignments simultaneously, and optimizing your workflow is crucial for meeting deadlines and delivering quality work consistently.

Have a list of current projects and when their due dates are. From there, categorize them based on when you need to complete everything. Have a list of priorities and a list of non-priorities. Follow this list to ensure you never miss a deadline. Missing a deadline is the kiss of death for freelance writers. If a brand cannot trust you'll get a job done on time, they will most likely start looking for someone new to funnel their projects to.

Closer to the end of this book, we'll discuss the importance of financial planning and budgeting as a freelance writer. Irregular income patterns are common in freelancing, and learning to manage your finances prudently, including setting aside funds for taxes and emergencies, is essential for achieving long-term financial stability. Again, there's no more uneasy feeling than not seeing money coming into your business bank account and not knowing when the next time will be that you'll see something deposited. So, focus on building your income stream.

CHAPTER 8 SUMMARY AND KEY TAKEAWAYS

- Freelance writing offers opportunities to earn a substantial income, and content platforms are valuable for finding clients and projects.
- When choosing content platforms, consider your niche, preferred writing style, and platform types, such as job boards, content marketplaces, or self-publishing platforms.
- Craft a compelling profile on content marketplaces to attract potential clients, optimize it with relevant keywords, and showcase your portfolio.
- Effective bidding on projects involves tailoring proposals to individual client needs and highlighting your unique value proposition.
- Building long-term client relationships can lead to steady income, focusing on exceeding client expectations and delivering high-quality work consistently.
- Diversify your income sources by exploring various niches, project types, and client relationships.
- Implement time management strategies to balance multiple projects effectively and meet deadlines.
- Financial planning and budgeting are crucial for managing the irregular income patterns common in freelancing, including setting aside funds for taxes and emergencies to achieve long-term financial stability.

Chapter 9
Pitching to Clients and Publications

As you progress in your quest for a six-figure income as a writer, the ability to pitch effectively to potential clients and publications becomes an indispensable skill. This chapter looks at the art and science of pitching, offering insights into crafting compelling pitches, identifying suitable targets, and negotiating rates and contracts that align with your goals.

Crafting Effective Pitches

A well-crafted pitch is your gateway to landing lucrative writing assignments. It's your opportunity to demonstrate your value to potential clients and publications and convince them that you're the right writer for the job.

We'll begin by exploring the anatomy of an effective pitch. A strong pitch typically includes three key things:

1. A concise introduction that grabs the recipient's attention
2. A clear and compelling proposal that outlines the scope of the project
3. A persuasive conclusion that encourages a positive response.

The language and tone of each should align with the recipient's expectations and preferences.

Understanding your target audience is crucial when crafting pitches. Research the client or publication to grasp their needs, objectives, and preferences. Tailor your pitch to address their specific pain points and demonstrate how your skills and expertise can fulfill their requirements.

Moreover, you can't overlook the importance of personalization in pitches. Generic pitches rarely stand out, so taking the time to customize your pitch for each recipient can significantly improve your success rate. Highlighting your understanding of their industry or previous work and expressing genuine enthusiasm for the opportunity can make a substantial difference.

Pitching also involves demonstrating your credibility and expertise. Including a brief bio or portfolio of your relevant work can help establish your authority in the subject matter and boost your chances of being considered for the project.

Identifying Potential Clients and Publications

Effectively identifying potential clients and publications is the foundation of successful pitching. Targeting the right opportunities increases your chances of landing high-paying assignments that align with your expertise and interests.

Throughout this book, I've presented various strategies for prospecting and finding potential clients and publications in your niche. This includes utilizing online job boards and freelance marketplaces, subscribing to industry-specific publications, and networking with fellow writers and professionals. Building a robust list of leads is an ongoing process, and you should always maintain and expand your prospect list over time.

Once you've identified potential targets, conducting thorough research is essential. Dive deep into their websites, publications, or social media profiles to gain insights into their needs, style, and the type of content they value. The more you know about your target, the better you can tailor your pitch to resonate with their specific requirements.

Keeping your pipeline full is a must. You should never be sitting in front of your keyboard with no one to reach out to. Whatever your industry or niche, you should always be prospecting new business. That means creating a list of business names, contact names of the business, phone numbers, and email addresses.

In today's age, not many people will knock on doors to stir up business (and that's fine). However, you need to be willing to pick up the phone or send out emails to prospects, introducing yourself, exposing their potential pain points, and then explaining to them how you provide the solution.

Negotiating Rates and Contracts

Negotiating rates and contracts is a critical aspect of securing well-paying writing assignments. It's where you have the opportunity to define the terms of your work and ensure that the compensation aligns with your expertise and effort.

It's important that you set a competitive yet fair rate. Research industry standards and benchmarks to determine a rate that reflects your skills and experience. When negotiating, be prepared to articulate the value you bring to the project and how your expertise justifies your rate.

You should be prepared for pushback no matter what your rates are. Everyone will try to talk you down lower, tell you they can go with "X" company for a cheaper price, and try to have you agree to their terms. You can absolutely do that if you need the money. But one thing to consider is you need to be self-aware of your worth. How much value does your writing bring to their business? What problem do you solve? Is it really a pricing issue? If they could get a better price from going with "X" company, why haven't they already done so?

Many companies and people you talk to will intentionally mislead you into thinking your pricing isn't competitive. If you've done your homework and created your rates based on what you found from the data, you already know your pricing is fair. You don't have to back down, but you also don't need to be aggressive with your counter or rebuttal. Simply explain to them that you understand their position and then, in a friendly manner, provide the reasons why you're the best at what you do and the value you bring.

You can also tell them if they would feel more comfortable, you can complete a few projects for them as a trial, and if they agree that the value is there and you get them the results they're looking for, you can continue working together. And if they don't find the value or results and you part ways, you now have things you know you need to work on, or you merely dodged a grenade of a client who is impossible to please and would be more of a headache than they're worth.

That said, it's crucial that you focus on the art of professional communication during negotiations. Politeness, clarity, and professionalism in your correspondence can foster positive relationships with clients and lead to successful negotiations.

When you and a prospect decide to work together, you need clear and comprehensive contracts. Contracts provide legal protection for both you and the client, outlining expectations, deliverables, timelines, and payment terms.

Payment terms are a crucial aspect of contract negotiation. You may choose upfront payments or milestone payments to ensure a consistent income flow and reduce the risk of non-payment.

Being that I'm not a lawyer and do not give out legal advice, your best bet is to either work with a lawyer to draft some writing contracts for you or, at a bare minimum, go online and find writing contract templates that you can (legally) use for your business. If you go the route of looking for a template online, be prepared to go in and make changes to the contract according to your terms, rates, etc.

But to simplify the entire process, it's much easier to work with a lawyer and allow them to produce something far better than you'll find online (and it will be completely customized for your writing business) to keep you legally protected.

CHAPTER 9 SUMMARY AND KEY TAKEAWAYS

- Effective pitching is essential for landing high-paying writing assignments and involves crafting compelling pitches that grab attention, outline project scope, and persuade recipients.
- The anatomy of a strong pitch includes a concise introduction, a clear proposal, and a persuasive conclusion tailored to the recipient's preferences.
- Research your target audience thoroughly to understand their needs and preferences, and personalize your pitches to demonstrate your understanding and enthusiasm.
- Identifying potential clients and publications involves ongoing prospecting, which includes using job boards, networking, and maintaining a robust list of leads.
- Negotiating rates and contracts is crucial for securing well-paying assignments, and you should research industry standards, articulate your value, and maintain professionalism during negotiations.
- Contracts are essential for legal protection and should outline expectations, deliverables, timelines, and payment terms. Consider seeking legal advice or using templates tailored to your writing business for contract creation.

Chapter 10
Leveraging Your Network

Earlier on in this book, I mentioned building and leveraging your network. This is one of the most powerful things you can do to help build your business and a six-figure income. In the dynamic world of writing, the adage "It's not just what you know, but who you know" holds significant weight. Some even say, "Your network is your net worth." All are true statements and ones I live by with my businesses.

Networking is a potent tool that can propel your writing career toward a six-figure income. This chapter explores the power of networking in the writing industry, strategies for building and maintaining valuable connections, and how to leverage referrals to secure high-paying gigs.

The Power of Networking in the Writing Industry

Networking is the art of building meaningful and mutually beneficial relationships within your industry. In the writing industry, where opportunities are often concealed behind closed doors, a robust network can open those doors and bring lucrative projects and collaborations to your doorstep.

We begin by understanding the immense value of networking. It's not just about the potential for job opportunities, it's about gaining insights, sharing knowledge, and fostering a sense of belonging within the writing community. Networking can provide access to mentors, peers, and clients who can offer guidance, support, and referrals.

In the digital age, online networking has become increasingly vital. Social media platforms, professional networks like LinkedIn, and writing communities offer opportunities to connect with fellow writers, editors, publishers, and potential clients. Building an online presence and participating in relevant forums can expand your reach and facilitate networking on a global scale.

If you underestimate the power of social media, you're missing the boat. It's vital that you build out an online presence where your audience lives. Create business pages where you can showcase your work, provide details on how people can contact you, and engage with your audience to help build attention toward your brand.

Strategies for Building and Maintaining Connections

Effective networking is not merely collecting business cards or LinkedIn connections — it's about cultivating genuine and enduring relationships. Let's look at some strategies for building and maintaining connections that can elevate your writing career and propel you closer to a six-figure income.

First, we have the art of the initial introduction. When reaching out to potential connections, whether in person or online, crafting a compelling and concise introduction that highlights your expertise and what you bring to the table is essential. Tailoring your message to the recipient's interests and needs can increase the chances of a positive response.

Networking events, both physical and virtual, are valuable opportunities to meet industry professionals and fellow writers. Some techniques for maximizing your impact at these events come from preparing thoughtful questions as well as active listening and follow-up following the events. Network with as many people as possible and exchange contact information with everyone you feel is valuable for both you and the other party.

Consistency is key to maintaining connections. Regularly engage with your network by sharing your insights, offering assistance, and participating in discussions. Your network should not feel like a one-way street where you only seek help, it should be a reciprocal exchange of knowledge and support for all parties involved.

Additionally, start building out your "inner circle." They say that you are the sum of those around you. To put it bluntly, if you hang out with five lazy individuals, you'll be the sixth. On the other hand, if you hang out with five high-performing individuals, you'll be the sixth. You never want to be the smartest person in the room. If you are, you're in the wrong room. Leveling up comes from surrounding yourself with people you aspire to be like.

Building a small group of trusted and supportive contacts can provide a deeper level of connection and collaboration. These relationships often lead to more substantial opportunities and a sense of camaraderie.

Using Referrals to Secure High-Paying Gigs

Referrals are the golden currency of networking in the writing industry. When a colleague or client vouches for your skills and professionalism, it carries significant weight.

It is in your best interest to leverage referrals to secure high-paying gigs. If someone says they were recommended to you by John Smith, if you blow them off or are not professional, that is also a reflection of John Smith. If John finds out that the person he referred was not taken care of, he will be less likely to refer more people to you.

First, we need to identify the importance of delivering exceptional work consistently. Satisfied clients and collaborators are more likely to refer you to others if they trust in the quality of your work. Building a reputation for reliability and excellence is the foundation for receiving referrals.

As mentioned earlier in this book, never miss a deadline. If there's no way you can meet the client's deadline, you need to immediately get on the phone with them and explain the situation so that when the deadline approaches, they don't become frustrated when you don't send them the completed project.

You should also explore the art of asking for referrals tactfully once you gain rapport with your clients. Your timing and approach are critical. It's essential to choose the right moment and ensure that your request is polite and considerate. Express your gratitude and make it easy for your contacts to refer you by providing the necessary information.

Something as simple as, "John, I truly appreciate your business and am humbled you put your trust in my skills to deliver the value you were looking for. I hope that this is a long-lasting relationship, as I enjoy working with you. In an effort to continue building my business, by chance, do you know of anyone who may also be in need of my services that you would be willing to refer me to?"

It should be a priority that you continually build referral relationships. Maintaining a strong rapport with those who have referred you in the past ensures that they continue to advocate for you in the future. Never do wrong by them. Regularly check in with them, express appreciation, and update them on your achievements and availability.

CHAPTER 10 SUMMARY AND KEY TAKEAWAYS

- Networking is a powerful tool for advancing your writing career, offering access to opportunities, mentorship, and support from peers and clients.
- Online networking, through platforms like LinkedIn and social media, is crucial for expanding your reach and connecting with industry professionals on a global scale.
- Effective networking involves crafting compelling introductions, actively participating in networking events, and consistently engaging with your network.
- Building an "inner circle" of trusted contacts can provide deeper connections and collaborative opportunities.
- Referrals are highly valuable in the writing industry, and delivering exceptional work consistently is essential for receiving referrals.
- Timing and tactful requests are crucial when asking for referrals from satisfied clients. Maintain strong relationships with those who have referred you in the past to ensure continued support and advocacy.

Part IV: Scaling Your Income

62

Chapter 11
Building Your 6-Figure Income as a Writer

In this chapter, we'll explore the strategies and steps you can take to build a six-figure annual income as a writer. Whether you're a freelance writer, novelist, content creator, or any other kind of wordsmith, these principles can apply to you. We'll also provide you with a handy table to help you understand the number of clients you'd need and the rates you should charge to achieve that coveted six-figure income.

The Path to Six Figures

Earning a six-figure income as a writer is an achievable goal, I'm living proof. That said, it requires dedication, strategy, and a diversified approach. Here are some key steps to help you get there:

1. Specialize in High-Demand Niches

Identify lucrative niches where your writing skills are in high demand. Some areas, like technology, finance, healthcare, and marketing, often pay top dollar for quality content. Focusing on such niches can significantly boost your income potential.

2. Build an Impressive Portfolio

Invest time in creating a portfolio that showcases your best work. High-quality samples can help you attract better-paying clients. If you're a fiction writer, publish your work on platforms like Amazon Kindle or submit it to literary magazines to gain exposure and build your reputation.

If you prefer to self-publish books, I have had great success with Draft2Digital for eBooks and Findaway Voices for audiobooks. Both will take a percentage of sales, but they will do all the heavy lifting when it comes to getting your books out to retailers. They make the process simple and easy to follow.

3. Network and Market Yourself

As mentioned in the previous chapter, networking is crucial in the writing world. Attend conferences, join writing groups, and engage with professionals in your chosen niche. Utilize social media and professional platforms like LinkedIn to promote your services and connect with potential clients.

In all honesty, LinkedIn is the most undervalued social media platform out there. You should absolutely create a LinkedIn profile if you don't already have one.

4. Offer a Range of Services

Diversify your writing services to cater to different clients. This might include content writing, copywriting, technical writing, editing, and more. Offering a broader skill set can attract a wider range of clients willing to pay for your expertise.

5. Set Competitive Rates

It's impossible to provide you with rates in this book. As much as I'd like to help you kickstart your writing career with how much you should be charging, there are truly too many variables to look at and consider.

What I would recommend is that you research the market rates in your niche and price your services competitively. Remember that charging too little can undermine your credibility, while charging too much may deter potential clients. Aim for a balance that reflects your skills and experience.

Also, take note that the market dictates your value. If your work does not reflect your rates and people stop doing business with you, it may be time to swallow your pride and reevaluate how much you charge.

6. Deliver Exceptional Quality

Consistently deliver high-quality work to build a strong reputation. Satisfied clients are more likely to become repeat clients and refer you to others. Strive for excellence in every project you undertake. If anything, under-promise and over-deliver.

Note that it doesn't mean telling them you're going to do basic work for them. The last thing you want to do is sell yourself short with your pitch. But always go above and beyond for your clients.

7. Scale Your Business

As your client base grows, consider hiring additional writers or assistants to help with your workload. This allows you to take on more projects and increase your income potential. The reality is we all get the same 24 hours in a day. That only leaves so much time for you to productively be writing. If you get more work than you can handle, hiring additional writers may be necessary to hit the six-figure income you're striving for.

8. Track Your Finances

Keep meticulous records of your income and expenses. I would highly recommend you purchase some sort of accounting software like QuickBooks. This will help you manage your finances effectively and ensure you're on track to reach your six-figure income goal.

Also, it's imperative that you open up a dedicated business account with your bank as well as a dedicated business credit card to keep your business and personal transactions separated. If you fail to do so, the IRS could very well chew you up and spit you out during a potential audit. You don't want that hassle and headache, so it's crucial you have separate accounts.

The Six-Figure Income Table

Many people look at a six-figure income as a pipe dream. An unattainable number that only "the most highly successful" will ever see. They assume you need to be some sort of genius in order to achieve two commas in their income. This couldn't be further from the truth.

In order to achieve a six-figure income, you first need to reverse-engineer $100,000. I'm no math whiz, but this is precisely what I did in order to set goals for myself and my business to grow to where it is today.

To give you a clearer picture of what it takes to earn a six-figure income as a writer, here's a table that outlines how many clients you would need and how much you would need to charge them at varying levels of clients:

Number of Clients	Monthly Rate per Client	Annual Income
10	$840	$100,800
15	$560	$100,800
20	$425	$100,800
25	$335	$100,500

Not as bad as you imagined, right? Making six figures per year isn't difficult, it's simply a numbers game. When you break it down as shown in the chart, it shows you how to eat an elephant — one bite at a time.

Granted, you aren't going to start your business on day one with ten or more clients. It could take you several months to achieve these numbers. But through networking and applying the strategies mentioned in this book it makes that challenge much more manageable and attainable. To circle back to what I said in the introduction of this book, nothing works unless you do. You need to be willing to continually work on growing your writing business.

The table illustrates that with just 10 clients, you'd need to charge each of them $840 per month to reach an annual six-figure income. Alternatively, you could have more clients at lower rates or fewer clients at higher rates — it all depends on your niche, skills, and business strategy.

Remember that building a six-figure income as a writer requires time, effort, and persistence. Stay committed to refining your craft, marketing your services, and delivering outstanding results, and you'll be well on your way to financial success in the world of writing.

In the next chapter, we'll explore advanced strategies for expanding your writing business and maximizing your income potential.

67

CHAPTER 11 SUMMARY AND KEY TAKEAWAYS

- Achieving a six-figure income as a writer is attainable through dedication, strategy, and diversification of your writing services.
- To boost your income potential, specialize in high-demand niches where your writing skills are in demand, such as technology, finance, healthcare, or marketing.
- Develop an impressive portfolio that showcases your best work and attracts better-paying clients.
- Network actively, attend conferences, join writing groups, and utilize social media, especially LinkedIn, to promote your services and connect with potential clients.
- Diversify your services to cater to different clients, offering content writing, copywriting, technical writing, editing, and more to attract a broader range of clients.
- Set competitive rates based on research in your niche, finding a balance that reflects your skills and experience.
- Deliver consistently high-quality work, strive for excellence, and aim to exceed client expectations.
- As your client base grows, consider scaling your business by hiring additional writers or assistants to take on more projects.
- Keep meticulous financial records, use accounting software, and maintain separate business accounts to manage your finances effectively.
- Use the table provided in this chapter to understand how many clients you would need and the rates you should charge to achieve a six-figure income, making it a manageable and attainable goal for your writing business.

Chapter 12

Passive Income Streams

Now that you understand a six-figure income isn't as difficult as you may have thought, let's dive into diversifying revenue sources beyond your traditional writing assignments. In this chapter, we explore the world of passive income streams for writers — ways to generate income continuously, even when you're not actively writing for clients. Or, as I like to say, generate income even while you're sleeping. That sounds great, right? We'll look at the processes of creating and selling eBooks, leveraging the power of blogging and affiliate marketing, and monetizing your expertise through online courses and webinars.

Creating and Selling eBooks

eBooks have revolutionized the publishing landscape, offering writers an accessible and lucrative avenue to showcase their expertise and creativity. In this section, we explore the process of creating and selling eBooks as a sustainable passive income stream.

We begin by discussing the advantages of eBooks as a source of passive income. eBooks are cost-effective to produce, have no printing or distribution costs, and can reach a global audience through digital platforms. This makes them an attractive option for writers looking to generate income beyond traditional writing assignments.

The first step in creating eBooks is selecting your niche and topic. You'll want to identify subjects that align with your expertise and audience's interests. It's essential to conduct market research and assess competition to determine the demand for your chosen topic.

The process of writing and formatting eBooks is next on your journey. You will want to figure out how you'll structure your eBook, craft compelling content, and design an engaging cover that will grab the attention of potential readers. Formatting considerations for various e-reader platforms can be somewhat tricky as each one may have different formatting requirements. By simply looking at their guidelines, they'll tell you exactly how to format your eBook, which tends to be very easy and basic.

Publishing and distribution are crucial aspects of the eBook creation process. One option to explore is self-publishing platforms like Amazon Kindle Direct Publishing (KDP), which empowers writers to publish and distribute their eBooks globally. You'll want to look at pricing strategies and marketing tactics to maximize sales and revenue. What are other similar books going for? Find that sweet spot in the middle, and that tends to be a safe spot to be.

If you want to go the route of KDP, the direct link to their website is:

www.KDP.amazon.com

Additionally, as mentioned in the previous chapter, if you prefer to self-publish books, I have had great success with Draft2Digital for eBooks and Findaway Voices for audiobooks. Both of these platforms will take a percentage of sales, but they will do all the heavy lifting when it comes to getting your books out to retailers. They make the process simple and easy to follow. I have had offers to work with different publishers, but the two I mentioned are so good that I've had no reason to make a change or jump ship.

If you're interested in these two options, their websites are:

www.Draft2Digitial.com

www.FindawayVoices.com

To sustain passive income from eBooks, it's your job to go out there and promote your titles. This can be done on social media and even through email blasts if you create an email list from your website. If you go through Draft2Digital and Findaway Voices, they provide you with opportunities to have promotions each month on one or more of your titles.

While many people think passive income means you don't need to do any work to make money, to get the biggest return, you will want to continually ensure you're getting your books out in front of people's faces to keep the sales and commissions coming in monthly.

It's not out of the question to make hundreds if not thousands of dollars through eBooks and audiobooks each month (depending on how many you publish and the demand for each title). If you produce a book that solves people's pain points or helps improve their lives or businesses in some way, it could very easily go viral, becoming an incredibly lucrative stream of passive income.

Blogging, Affiliate Marketing, and Ad Revenue

Blogging has evolved into a powerful platform for writers to express their thoughts, share knowledge, and generate passive income through affiliate marketing and ad revenue. In this section, we explore how you can harness the potential of blogging to leverage passive income through affiliate marketing and ad placement.

We begin by discussing the role of blogging as a vehicle for showcasing your expertise and building an online presence. A successful blog can attract a dedicated readership, which forms the foundation for affiliate marketing and ad opportunities.

Affiliate Marketing

Affiliate marketing is a method where writers promote products or services on their blog, earning a commission for each sale or action generated through their referral.

The art of content creation is pivotal in blogging and affiliate marketing. You will need to craft valuable, informative, and engaging blog posts that resonate with your audience and drive traffic to your affiliate partners. Balancing informative content with promotional content is essential to maintain credibility and reader trust.

There are several platforms out there you can leverage for affiliate sales and commission. Some of the best platforms out there are:

- ClickBank (www.clickbank.com)
- ShareASale (www.shareasale.com)
- Commission Junction (www.cj.com)
- Impact (www.impact.com)
- Amazon Associates (www.affilate-progam.amazon.com)

The key to leveraging these platforms is finding products or brands that resonate not only with your content but also with the potential reader. For instance, if you're writing content about the importance of using a protein powder post-workout, you wouldn't want to include an affiliate link to an LED lightbulb. You'd want to find an affiliate that sells protein powder and include that in your content to help convert sales.

Don't overdo your affiliates, though. I would only recommend using one affiliate link per piece of content. If you do too many, your content starts to look spammy, and it will turn the reader off as they will assume you're only looking to make a commission check.

Something you need to consider is your posting schedule. If you choose to post only one article per week, that's a great start. However, if you can publish multiple pieces of content each week on your website or blog, you can drastically increase your potential affiliate revenue.

We also discuss the significance of transparency and disclosure in affiliate marketing. Ethical practices, such as clearly disclosing affiliate relationships, are crucial for building and maintaining trust with your readers.

Monetizing your blog through affiliate marketing involves strategically placing affiliate links and calls to action. You should look at optimizing your content for conversions while ensuring a seamless and non-disruptive reader experience.

Ad Revenue

You can generate passive income through ad revenue by monetizing your blog content using platforms like Google AdSense and Ezoic. Ad networks have strict policies regarding content, placement, and user experience. Familiarize yourself with these guidelines to avoid issues with your ad revenue streams.

Before thinking about ad revenue, focus on creating valuable and engaging content. High-quality content attracts more visitors and keeps them on your site longer, increasing the potential for ad clicks.

Consider selecting a niche that is both personally interesting to you and has a good audience base. Popular niches often attract more advertisers, leading to higher ad rates.

Building a loyal and engaged audience is crucial for ad revenue. Promote your content through social media, email newsletters, and other marketing strategies to increase your website's traffic.

Ensure your website is user-friendly, mobile-responsive, and loads quickly. A well-optimized site can lead to better ad performance and higher rankings in search engines.

Proper ad placement is key. Make sure ads are visible but not intrusive. Common positions for ads include the header, sidebar, and within the content. Advertisements that blend well with your site's design tend to perform better.

Test different ad formats, sizes, and styles to see which ones work best for your audience. Some ad formats may perform better on certain devices or pages.

With the growing use of mobile devices, ensure that your site and ads are mobile-friendly. Responsive design and mobile ad units can boost your revenue.

Regularly review your ad performance metrics, such as click-through rates (CTR), RPM (revenue per thousand impressions), and EPMV (earnings per thousand visitors). Use this data to make informed decisions and optimize ad placements.

There are three platforms that tend to be the most recommended ad networks out there:

- Google Adsense (www.adsense.google.com)
- Ezoic (www.ezoic.com)
- Media.net (www.media.net)

Google AdSense is one of the most popular ad networks. Sign up, and Google will place relevant ads on your site. They offer a variety of ad formats, including display ads, text ads, and responsive ads.

Ezoic is an ad management platform that uses artificial intelligence to optimize ad placements and improve revenue. It's known for its ability to increase ad earnings without compromising user experience.

Media.net is another popular alternative to AdSense, particularly for bloggers. It focuses on contextual advertising and offers a range of ad formats.

Something to take into consideration is that it may take some time for you to build up a substantial income from ad revenue. Be patient, focus on providing value to your audience, and continuously optimize your approach to maximize your passive income from ads.

Online Courses and Webinars

Leveraging your expertise to create and sell online courses and webinars is another avenue for generating passive income as a writer. In this section, we explore the process of developing and marketing online educational content.

We begin by discussing the benefits of online courses and webinars. They allow you to share your knowledge, skills, and insights with a global audience, positioning you as an authority in your niche. Unlike traditional teaching, online courses and webinars enable you to reach a larger audience and generate income continuously.

Identifying your niche and target audience is the first step in creating online courses and webinars. You need to determine what topics and formats will resonate with your audience and align with your expertise.

The process of course creation involves structuring your content, developing engaging materials, and designing a compelling learning experience. It's important that you strategically plan and organize your course, choosing the right delivery platform, and creating high-quality content.

Speaking of delivery platforms, here are some of the most well-known and recommended platforms to consider hosting your online courses and webinars:

- Kajabi (www.kajabi.com)
- Udemy (www.udemy.com)
- Skillshare (www.skillshare.com)
- Teachable (www.teachable.com)
- Thinkific (www.thinkific.com)

Each of the above has its own advantages and disadvantages. Without knowing the direction you're going with your online courses or webinars, I would recommend going to each of their respective websites and learning what they are all about, and deciding based on what makes the most sense for your wants and needs.

Marketing your online courses and webinars is crucial for attracting participants and generating income. You should explore promoting your educational content through email marketing, social media, and partnerships. Building a reputation as an expert in your field can also boost enrollment and further help build your brand.

Monetization models for online courses and webinars, including one-time purchases, subscriptions, and memberships, are a great way to help you build your six-figure income. You can also look at different pricing strategies, discounts, and payment processing options with your online courses and seminars to help maximize your revenue potential.

CHAPTER 12 SUMMARY AND KEY TAKEAWAYS

- Generating passive income as a writer involves diversifying revenue sources beyond traditional assignments.
- Creating and selling eBooks is a cost-effective way to earn passive income, and platforms like Amazon Kindle Direct Publishing (KDP), Draft2Digital, and Findaway Voices provide accessible publishing options.
- To succeed with eBooks, choose niches that align with your expertise, conduct market research, and create high-quality content. Effective promotion is essential to sustain income from eBooks.
- Blogging can be a powerful platform for generating passive income through affiliate marketing and ad revenue. High-quality, valuable content attracts readers and forms the foundation for monetization.
- In affiliate marketing, select products or services relevant to your content and audience, create content that balances information with promotion, and ensure transparency and disclosure to maintain reader trust.
- Ad revenue from platforms like Google AdSense, Ezoic, and Media.net can provide passive income. Optimize your blog for user experience, proper ad placement, and mobile-friendliness to maximize ad earnings.
- Online courses and webinars are opportunities to monetize your expertise. Identifying your niche, creating high-quality educational content, and selecting the right delivery platform are key steps.
- Marketing online courses and webinars through email marketing, social media, partnerships, and building an expert reputation can attract participants and generate income.
- Explore different monetization models, pricing strategies, and payment processing options to maximize revenue potential from your online courses and webinars.

Chapter 13
Building Your Personal Brand

In the ever-evolving landscape of the writing industry, building a personal brand has become an indispensable tool for writers seeking to establish authority, expand their reach, and unlock new opportunities. This chapter explores the art of crafting and nurturing your personal brand as a writer, guiding you through the process of establishing authority in your niche, monetizing your personal brand, and striking the delicate balance between branding and authenticity.

Establishing Authority in Your Niche

Establishing authority in your niche is a cornerstone of building a personal brand as a writer. It involves positioning yourself as an expert, thought leader, or go-to source in a specific field. Let's look at some of the strategies and tactics to help you claim your rightful place as an authority figure in your niche.

The journey begins with niche selection. You need to be sure to identify a niche that aligns with your interests, expertise, and market demand. Selecting the right niche is essential as it forms the foundation of your personal brand and influences your ability to stand out in a crowded market.

Creating high-quality content is paramount to establishing authority. Strive to consistently produce valuable, insightful content that showcases your expertise and resonates with your target audience. This includes crafting blog posts, articles, videos, or other formats that educate, inform, and engage your audience.

Building a content calendar and strategy is the next step in your authority-building journey. Plan your content to address your niche's most pressing questions and challenges. Consistency in content creation and delivery is essential for maintaining and growing your authority over time.

Leveraging social media and online communities is another key aspect of establishing authority. As mentioned earlier throughout this book, you should be using platforms like LinkedIn, Twitter, and industry-specific forums to share your content, engage with your audience, and connect with peers and influencers in your niche.

Networking and collaboration also play a crucial role in authority-building. The benefits of forming partnerships, guest posting on authoritative websites, and participating in joint projects are a great way to expand your reach and credibility within your niche.

When building your personal brand, don't ask people to buy anything just yet. Gary Vaynerchuk puts this into perspective with his book "Jab, Jab, Jab, Right Hook." If you haven't read that book yet, you should add it to your list. In fact, do yourself a favor and read everything Gary has published, they're all full of golden nuggets you can implement into your writing business and life.

Your top priority should be to bring value to your niche. When just starting out, you should not have an ask. Don't ask people to do anything other than hope they get value from your content. When you continually build value, and people are engaging with you, over time, start throwing in an ask. Ask them to sign up for your newsletter. Ask them to check out your book or course. But tossing it in too early may turn people away if they don't see value in what you're doing or see value in you as an authoritative leader in the niche.

Monetizing Your Personal Brand

Monetizing your personal brand is a natural progression once you've established authority in your niche. This section dives into various methods and strategies to turn your personal brand into a sustainable source of income.

One of the primary avenues for monetizing your personal brand is through sponsored content and partnerships. You should explore ways that you can identify suitable brands and businesses to collaborate with, negotiate terms, and create sponsored content that aligns with your brand and provides value to your audience.

Transparency in sponsored content and partnerships must be emphasized to maintain trust with your audience. Disclose relationships with brands or businesses while delivering sponsored content that aligns with your brand and provides value to your audience.

Affiliate marketing (as mentioned earlier in this book) is another income-generating strategy. Identify and promote relevant affiliate products or services that resonate with your audience. Ethical practices and transparent disclosures are emphasized to maintain trust with your followers.

Creating and selling your products or services is a direct method of monetization. Develop and create eBooks, courses, workshops, or consulting services that cater to your audience's needs and interests.

Membership and subscription models are gaining traction as a way to monetize personal brands as well. You can do this through your website or even social media platforms now have ways that people can subscribe to "exclusive" paid content. The goal to make this profitable is to build exclusive communities or content libraries for subscribers that bring value so you can leverage the advantages of recurring revenue streams.

Engaging in public speaking, workshops, or coaching services can also be lucrative extensions of your personal brand. Identify speaking opportunities, set speaking fees, and deliver compelling presentations or training sessions that add massive value to those who pay to engage with you.

Balancing Branding with Authenticity

Balancing branding with authenticity is a delicate but essential aspect of nurturing your personal brand. Authenticity is the core of a strong personal brand, and you must maintain it while strategically managing your image.

The first thing to touch on is discussing the importance of staying true to your values and beliefs. Authenticity is rooted in your genuine voice, opinions, and experiences. It's crucial to align your personal brand with what you truly believe and stand for. Real recognizes real, and fakes generally get exposed. Just be your authentic self.

Consistency in branding is essential, but it should not come at the expense of authenticity. Create a consistent brand image while allowing room for evolution and growth. Authenticity lies in being transparent about your journey and experiences.

Managing feedback and criticism is another aspect of balancing branding with authenticity. You should respond to both positive and negative feedback in a way that upholds your personal brand's integrity and authenticity. If you're someone who doesn't take criticism very well or has a short fuse, I would recommend not replying to negative feedback at all.

Something that I like to tell everyone I work with, and I think it's important for you to understand, is that no one who's doing better than you is going to be leaving you negative remarks or trying to put you down. It's generally the people below you who feel the need to be negative in order to try and tear you down to their level.

Now, constructive criticism is something different. If someone has analyzed what you're doing and is trying to give you advice to help you grow, don't brush it off. Take in the constructive criticism and use it to make yourself, your personal brand, and your writing business better.

CHAPTER 13 SUMMARY AND KEY TAKEAWAYS

- Building a personal brand is crucial for writers to establish authority, expand their reach, and unlock new opportunities in the evolving writing industry.
- Establishing authority in your niche involves niche selection, consistently creating high-quality content, building a content calendar, leveraging social media, and networking and collaborations.
- Prioritize providing value to your audience before asking them to buy anything. Continually build value and authority in your niche to gain trust over time.
- Monetizing your personal brand can be achieved through sponsored content, affiliate marketing, creating and selling products or services, public speaking, and membership or subscription models.
- Maintain transparency in sponsored content and partnerships to preserve trust with your audience. Promote affiliate products or services that align with your audience's interests and provide value.
- Balance branding with authenticity by staying true to your values and beliefs, maintaining consistency in branding while allowing room for growth, and managing feedback and criticism in a way that upholds your personal brand's integrity.
- Constructive criticism can be valuable for growth, but negative feedback from individuals who are not doing better should not deter you from your path. Use constructive criticism to improve your personal brand and writing business.

Part V: Managing Your Writing Career

Chapter 14
Time Management and Productivity

As it relates to writing, you only have 24 hours on any given day. Many question how it's possible that I can write upwards of six articles a day for my website or my clients. It all comes down to time management and productivity. I don't have some secret formula that will multiply your results. Only you can determine how you spend your days. In the realm of writing, where deadlines are constant companions and creativity must flow consistently, mastering time management and productivity is paramount. I've fine-tuned my schedule and time management to be as productive as possible. In this chapter, I will uncover the art of optimizing your writing time, conquering procrastination, and leveraging tools to enhance your efficiency and output. There's no time to waste, let's get into it.

Effective Writing Schedules

Effective writing schedules are the cornerstone of productive writing habits. This section explores the importance of structuring your day to maximize your creative and productive potential.

We begin by discussing the significance of understanding your personal circadian rhythm. Everyone has a biological clock that dictates their most productive and creative periods during the day. Only you can identify your peak hours and align your writing tasks with them for optimal results. For some people, the morning hours are their most productive time. For others, it's at night. Whichever works best for you is where you should leverage your creative genius.

Creating a dedicated writing space is the next step in crafting an effective writing schedule. It's important that you have a workspace that is conducive to focus and creativity. That means zero distractions. Be sure your workspace is clutter-free, organized, and an inspiring writing environment.

Consistency is key to building effective writing schedules. The value of establishing daily, weekly, or monthly writing routines is paramount to your success in achieving a six-figure income from writing. Regular writing habits help train your brain to get into the writing flow more easily and enhance your overall productivity.

Setting specific writing goals is pivotal in effective time management. Break down larger writing projects into manageable tasks and set achievable milestones. This approach prevents you from feeling overwhelmed and provides a clear roadmap for your writing endeavors.

Prioritization is also a crucial skill in time management. Identify high-priority writing tasks and address them first to ensure progress and productivity. Time blocking and to-do lists are practical tools for managing your workload effectively.

Beating Procrastination

Procrastination is a common foe of writers, often lurking in the shadows and hindering progress. It's imperative that you understand what is causing your procrastination and effectively manage it.

The first task is finding the root causes of procrastination. Understanding the psychological factors, such as fear of failure, perfectionism, or lack of motivation, can help you identify and address the specific triggers of your procrastination tendencies.

The Pomodoro Technique is introduced as a powerful tool for beating procrastination. This time management method involves breaking your work into focused intervals (typically 25 minutes) followed by short breaks. This technique, when implemented, can enhance your concentration and productivity.

Tackling writer's block is a common challenge for writers. It's common for writers to have moments where they are simply out of their flow and where creativity suffers. Rather than getting frustrated, you need to view writer's block as a temporary hiccup rather than an insurmountable barrier. As with most things, this too shall pass. Techniques for overcoming writer's block, such as freewriting, mind mapping, and changing your writing environment, are great ways to get your creative juices flowing again.

Something else to look at is your accountability. No one is going to hold your hand or give you a pat on the butt. Accountability is a potent weapon against procrastination. You need to be able to hold yourself to a higher standard than mediocrity. If you want to hit a six-figure income, it'll never happen without accountability and showing up every day, even when you don't want to sit in front of your screen and keyboard.

Tools for Efficient Writing

In the digital age, numerous tools and software are available to streamline your writing process and boost your efficiency. Let's take a look at some essential tools and their applications in enhancing your writing productivity.

We begin by discussing word processing software, such as Microsoft Word and Google Docs. These tools offer features like spell-check, formatting options, and cloud storage, making them indispensable for writing and organizing your work.

Writing productivity apps are introduced as valuable aids for staying on track. Tools like Trello, Evernote, and Asana for task management, note-taking, and project organization are great ways for you to jot down ideas or things you need to get done in your daily workflow. These apps can help you stay organized and efficient in your writing projects. Even writing notes down using pen and paper are acceptable ways of accomplishing this. I often joke that I have a great memory, it's just short. You may relate. Without using these tools, some of my best ideas and work may have never been published. Don't say you'll write it down later, do it now.

Grammar and proofreading tools are essential for polishing your work. Sure, you could use the spell-check function in Microsoft Word or Google Docs, but the use of specific tools like Grammarly, ProWritingAid, and Hemingway Editor are great for catching grammatical errors, improving writing style, and enhancing readability. I highly recommend you use these tools in your writing to make it more polished and professional.

Distraction-blocking software, such as Freedom and Cold Turkey, can be an excellent way for you to overcome digital distractions. These tools can help you stay focused during your dedicated writing sessions and help you stay on task and productive.

Time-tracking apps can also be implemented for assessing and optimizing your writing time. Tools like Toggl and Clockify for monitoring your work hours, identifying time sinks, and improving your overall time management can help improve your productivity throughout the day.

Kill All Distractions

You would be amazed at how much time you waste throughout the day without realizing it. I first noticed this when the iPhone started showing screen time within the settings. I was shocked at where my time was spent each day. It was at that moment I realized that my phone was holding me back from being even more productive than I already was.

To help you stay focused and make your way toward a six-figure income, try implementing these strategies to kill all distractions.

Stop Using Social Media Throughout the Day

It was shown that Millennials check their phones over 150 times per day. Talk about a productivity killer. If what you're doing on your phone is not business-related, stay off your phone. Many people grab their phone to check something, then decide to quickly look at their notifications on social media. Before they know it, they've gone down a rabbit hole that pulled them away from the work they should be completing.

The best thing for you to do is to stay off social media during the day. Sure, you may need to post something for your business on your business pages but don't get sucked in. In fact, to eliminate the need to even go into your social platforms, I use and recommend software called Buffer that allows me to go in and draft all of my social media posts and schedule them to post automatically without me needing to go into each platform and do so. This not only saves me a bunch of time but also prevents me from getting sucked into the black hole that's social media.

Put Your Phone into "DO NOT DISTURB" Mode

I found that if you don't value your time, no one else will. How many times do you check your email or texts to see if someone reached out to you? More times than not, if anything is in your inboxes, it's because someone wants your time. But who owns your time? You or them? If you value your time, you will maximize it by staying productive and not pulling yourself away to see who is dinging your phone.

If I wanted to stay as productive as possible with my writing, I couldn't be bothered by the all too common rings, dings, and buzzes of my phone. I used to always have it sitting next to me, and as soon as a notification would come in, I'd grab my phone as if I needed to put a fire out immediately. What a waste of time. I'd totally lose my flow with my writing, and it would take me a good 15 minutes to get back in such a state.

The best thing I found to do is simply put my phone in "do not disturb" mode. I kept a few important contacts on bypass, such as family, large accounts, and close friends and neighbors. Other than those who I allowed to bypass the "do not disturb" mode, everyone else would need to sit tight until I was free.

I can only speak for myself, but I believe you should have the same mindset that nobody respects my time more than me. If someone needs to speak with me, they need to get on my calendar and set up a call. Random phone calls will no longer be accepted. You may look at this as being rude, but it again comes down to the fact that I respect my time and want to maximize every second I can during the workday.

Close Your Email

Another time-sucker I was dealing with was my email. As soon as an email came in, I felt like I needed to reply within seconds to show that I was "on top of my business." The truth is, those who emailed me were just as busy as I was and didn't need an immediate reply.

What I found useful was only checking my email a couple of times throughout the workday. This prevented me from constantly looking over at one of my external monitors to see if anything new came into my inbox. If you currently have a business, you know what fills up your inbox more than anything else — SPAM. I found I was constantly checking email only to delete 90% of what came in. So, I did away with it all and only checked my inbox twice a day.

Each time that I set aside to check my email, I'd focus solely on getting through each pressing email and then deleting the spam and emails that did not require my attention or a reply. Also, don't be afraid to unsubscribe from newsletters that no longer provide you with value or send spammy emails into your junk folder so that they don't pop up and cause you to think the email needs your attention.

Turn off the Radio and Television

The last strategy I would recommend is for those who "need background noise." While you may think it helps keep you productive or in your flow, the fact is that you subconsciously are listening and paying attention to each song and word. Think about if one of your favorite songs comes on or whatever is on the television is an update that piques your interest — you're paying attention to the words or what's being said, even if you aren't looking directly at the source. This can take you out of your flow.

Turn everything off and work in silence. You don't need to be jamming in the office to keep your spirits lifted. If you need that kind of stimulus to get you through the workday, perhaps what you're doing isn't truly your interest or passion. To stay dialed in, you need to remain focused and productive. Outside auditory noises are a distraction and can turn productive workflow into an office dance party. The best thing for you to do is turn it all off and eliminate all noises and distractions.

Sort of a shameless plug, but if you want to learn more about how to be as productive as possible, please check out my book titled "The Productivity

Playbook." It's one of my best-sellers and something I recommend everyone read to maximize their day.

CHAPTER 14 SUMMARY AND KEY TAKEAWAYS

- Time management and productivity are essential skills for writers, given the constant presence of deadlines and the need for consistent creativity.
- Effective writing schedules should align with your personal circadian rhythm, create a dedicated writing space free of distractions, establish consistent writing routines, set specific goals, and prioritize tasks using time blocking and to-do lists.
- Procrastination can be tackled by understanding its root causes, implementing techniques like the Pomodoro Technique for focused work intervals, and overcoming writer's block using methods such as freewriting and changing your writing environment.
- Accountability is crucial in maintaining productivity, and holding yourself to a higher standard is necessary to achieve a six-figure income as a writer.
- Productivity tools, including word processing software, writing productivity apps, grammar and proofreading tools, distraction-blocking software, and time-tracking apps, can streamline the writing process and enhance efficiency.
- To kill distractions, avoid social media during work hours, put your phone in "do not disturb" mode, limit email checking to specific times, and work in silence without background noise.
- Maximizing productivity is essential for achieving success, and resources like my "The Productivity Playbook" can provide valuable insights into improving your efficiency and time management skills.

Chapter 15
Handling Finances

When building out your writing business, handling finances wisely is a crucial aspect that often goes overlooked. This chapter dives deep into the realm of personal finance for writers, guiding you through the essentials of budgeting and managing your income, understanding the intricacies of taxes for freelance writers, and planning for a secure financial future through saving and investing.

Budgeting and Managing Income

Budgeting is the cornerstone of financial stability and success. It involves a comprehensive understanding of your income, expenses, and financial goals. In this section, we explore the importance of budgeting and provide practical steps to effectively manage your income.

We begin by discussing the significance of tracking your income and expenses. Keeping a detailed record of your earnings and expenditures provides valuable insights into your financial habits and enables you to identify areas where you can make improvements.

Creating a budget is the next step in the financial journey on your way to a six-figure. You need to create a process of developing a personalized budget that aligns with your income and financial goals. Budgets help you allocate funds for essentials like bills and groceries while also setting aside money for savings and investments.

The big difference between running your writing business and working for someone is that you don't have an employer 401(k), any sort of matching program, or an investment plan through the company you work for. Essentially, you're on your own, and creating a SEP fund or IRA is necessary for your retirement and financial future.

Managing irregular income is a common challenge for freelance writers. You will need to explore strategies for handling variable income streams, such as setting aside a portion of each payment for taxes and creating a financial buffer for lean months where you may not be bringing in as much money as in previous months.

Emergency funds are a critical component of financial security. You need to take into account the importance of building an emergency fund to cover unexpected expenses like medical bills or equipment repairs.

Debt management is another essential aspect of handling finances. You must be able to manage and reduce debt, including prioritizing high-interest debts and exploring consolidation options.

Overall, I must preface all of this by saying I am not an accountant, CPA, or financial advisor. I'm not giving you financial advice, and I would highly recommend you work with a CPA not only for your business but to help manage your own personal finances for yourself and your family.

Taxes for Freelance Writers

Understanding taxes is paramount for freelance writers, as you are responsible for managing your tax obligations. In this section, I'll help demystify the complexities of taxes and provide guidance on navigating the tax landscape as a freelance writer based on my experiences and knowledge from tackling my own head-on.

We begin by discussing the importance of tracking income and expenses for tax purposes. Maintaining accurate records is crucial for calculating your taxable income and maximizing deductions. This is where something like QuickBooks is a valuable asset as it can create reports and give you a visual of where you were, are, and the potential future outlook.

We'll explore the types of taxes that freelance writers may encounter, including income tax, self-employment tax, and state taxes. Understanding the tax obligations in your location is essential for compliance. This entire section is more of an overview, and you should absolutely do some research on what tax obligations you have in your area or get with a qualified CPA who can help you navigate these somewhat murky waters.

Tax deductions and credits are valuable tools for reducing your tax liability. There are several common deductions and credits available to freelance writers, such as home office deductions, business expenses, mileage, and retirement contributions.

Quarterly tax payments are a unique requirement for self-employed individuals. It's important to understand the process of making quarterly estimated tax payments to the IRS, including calculating the amounts and staying compliant with deadlines.

There are deadlines that need to be met for quarterly taxes, and having them in your calendar can help prevent you from missing these key dates for your business tax obligations.

Quarterly estimated taxes follow the payment period outlined below. Please note that these dates are approximate, and it's essential to verify the exact due dates with the relevant tax authorities, as they may change from year to year.

Payment Period	Due Date
Q1: Jan. 1 - Mar. 31	Apr. 15
Q2: Apr. 1 - May 31	Jun. 15
Q3: Jun. 1 - Aug. 31	Sept. 15
Q4: Sept. 1 - Dec. 31	Jan. 15

These due dates are typical for federal income tax in the United States for individuals and small businesses, but it's essential to check with your specific tax authority or consult with a tax professional for the most accurate and up-to-date information regarding your tax obligations.

Hiring a tax professional is often a wise choice for freelance writers, especially as your income and tax obligations become more complex.

Saving and Investing for the Future

Planning for a secure financial future is a key aspect of financial well-being. In this section, we explore strategies for saving and investing to achieve your long-term financial goals.

We begin by discussing the importance of setting clear financial goals. Whether you aim to buy a home, fund your children's education, or retire comfortably, having defined objectives is crucial for creating a financial plan.

Savings strategies should be explored, including setting up automated savings accounts, creating sinking funds for specific expenses, and prioritizing long-term savings goals like retirement.

Investing is a powerful tool for growing your wealth over time. You may wish to consider different investment options, such as stocks, bonds, mutual funds, and real estate. Understanding your risk tolerance and investment horizon is essential for making informed investment decisions.

Retirement planning is another critical component of securing your financial future. Strategies such as retirement accounts like IRAs and 401(k)s may be wise investment choices that align with your retirement goals. Again, consulting with a CPA or accountant would be a wise decision to ensure you set up a plan that aligns with your needs and goals over time.

Diversification is a critical principle in investing. Spreading your investments across different asset classes is crucial to mitigate risk and optimize returns.

CHAPTER 15 SUMMARY AND KEY TAKEAWAYS

- Managing finances is a critical aspect of running a successful writing business, and it involves budgeting, understanding taxes, and planning for the future.
- Budgeting starts with tracking your income and expenses, creating a personalized budget, managing irregular income, building an emergency fund, and addressing debt management.
- Freelance writers must understand various taxes, including income tax, self-employment tax, and state taxes. Keeping accurate records, utilizing tax deductions and credits, and making quarterly estimated tax payments are essential for tax compliance.
- Hiring a tax professional becomes increasingly important as your income and tax obligations become more complex.
- Saving and investing for the future involves setting clear financial goals, using savings strategies like automated accounts and sinking funds, considering different investment options, and planning for retirement through accounts like IRAs and 401(k)s.
- Diversifying your investments across various asset classes is crucial for risk management and optimizing returns in the long term. Consulting with financial professionals is advisable for personalized financial planning.

Chapter 16
Final Thoughts

As you reach the closing chapter of "Write Your Way to a 6-Figure Income," it's time to pause, reflect, and chart the course moving forward. This chapter serves as a moment of introspection, goal-setting, and a source of encouragement for your writing journey.

Reflecting on Your Writing Journey

Before embarking on the final leg of your writing journey, it's essential to take a moment to reflect on how far you've come. Consider the valuable insights you've gained from the preceding chapters, the skills you've honed, and the knowledge you've acquired about the writing industry, mindset, and business aspects.

Reflecting on your writing journey is an opportunity to celebrate your achievements, no matter how small they may seem. Recognize the milestones you've reached, the challenges you've overcome, and the growth you've experienced as a writer. Your journey is a testament to your dedication and perseverance.

This moment of reflection also invites you to consider the changes you've made in your writing career. Have you developed a more growth-oriented mindset? Have you established a consistent writing routine? Are you taking steps to build your personal brand or increase your income? Acknowledging your progress is a source of motivation and inspiration for what lies ahead.

Setting and Achieving Your Six-Figure Writing Goals

With reflection as your compass, it's time to set your sights on the future and define your six-figure writing goals. Whether you've already begun your journey or are just starting out, having clear, ambitious goals is instrumental in charting your path to success.

Utilize the process of setting SMART goals — Specific, Measurable, Achievable, Relevant, and Time-Bound goals. By breaking down your aspirations into concrete, actionable steps, you can turn your dreams of a six-figure writing income into a reality.

Achieving your six-figure writing goals requires commitment and strategy. Create a roadmap that outlines the actions, resources, and timelines needed to reach your objectives. This roadmap serves as a guide for your ongoing journey, similar to that of a business plan, helping you stay on course even when faced with obstacles.

Along the way, remember the importance of resilience and adaptability. Your path to a six-figure writing income may not be without setbacks or detours. It's how you respond to these challenges and continue learning and growing that will define your success.

Encouragement and Final Words

As you close the pages of this book, know that you are not alone in your writing journey. Many writers, like myself, have walked a similar path and faced similar challenges.

In this book, I've shared my own stories, insights, and encouragement to remind you that your goals are achievable and your dreams are within reach. They offer advice on navigating the ups and downs of the writing industry, overcoming self-doubt, and finding fulfillment in your craft.

In these final words, remember that your writing journey is unique, and your path to a six-figure income is yours to create. Embrace the lessons learned, the skills acquired, and the opportunities that lie ahead. The world of writing is vast and ever-evolving, and your potential as a writer is boundless.

As you move forward, keep this book as a reference, a source of inspiration, and a reminder of the path you've chosen. Your journey as a writer is a testament to your passion, creativity, and determination. With the knowledge, mindset, and strategies you've acquired, you are well-equipped to write your way to a six-figure income and beyond.

Congratulations on embarking on this transformative journey. Your story as a successful writer is just beginning, and the world eagerly awaits the words you'll share and the impact you'll make. Here's to a future filled with creativity, success, and fulfillment as you continue to write your way to the six-figure income you've envisioned for yourself.

How to Stay in Touch with the Author

As you turn the last page of this book, I want to express my heartfelt gratitude for choosing to embark on this literary journey with me to help you earn a six-figure income through writing. Your support means the world to me, and I hope the words within these pages have provided you with the blueprint to get started as a writer.

Writing this book has been a labor of love, a culmination of countless hours of research, reflection, and creativity. This is a way for me to take my 20+ years as a writer and help those who want to paint a new life for themselves through writing. It has been a privilege to share my thoughts, stories, and ideas with you, and I sincerely hope that they have resonated with you on a deep and meaningful level.

Our connection and work doesn't have to end here. I would love to stay in touch and learn about how the pages in this book have helped you build the six-figure income you envisioned for yourself. You can follow me on social media, where I often share my thoughts, insights, and glimpses into my daily life and writing:

Twitter: WeikFitness

Instagram: WeikFitness

Facebook: WeikFitnessLLC or my personal account MattWeik.Fitness

LinkedIn: MattWeik

Additionally, you can also stay in touch by visiting my websites, www.WeikFitness.com, www.TheWritingRebels.com, and www.MattWeik.com. Feel free to subscribe to my weekly newsletter at WeikFitness.com, where you'll receive exclusive content, early access to my upcoming works, and the opportunity to participate in discussions with fellow readers.

I value your feedback and cherish the connections forged through our shared love of writing. Your reviews, comments, and messages inspire me to continue creating, exploring, and pushing the boundaries of content creation.

Remember, this book is just one chapter in the ongoing narrative of our connection. I look forward to many more adventures together through the written word. Thank you again for your support, and may your journey through life's pages be filled with joy, enlightenment, and endless wonder.

Also by Matt Weik

Personal Training Secrets: Don't Make These 35 Business Mistakes
No More Mistakes: Your Guide to Health and Fitness
The Secret to Success: Goal Setting in 4 Easy Steps
Prioritizing Your Health: A Guide to Getting Started
Entrepreneurial Business Success
Fit for Survival
Becoming Your Own G.O.A.T. : 15 Strategies to Win in Business and Life
The 20 C's That Create Success
Fit to Sell: A Guide to Staying Fit for the Sales Professional Whose Life
Involves Constant Travel
Raising Strong & Healthy Kids
The Productivity Playbook
Marketing 101 for Personal Trainers
F*ck Your Opinion: How to Shut Out the Noise, Stay Focused, and Dominate
Get Fit Now!
Write Your Way to a 6-Figure Income: Take Your Passion for Writing and
Build It into a Profitable Business

Watch for more at www.weikfitness.com.

About the Author

Matt Weik has been featured in over 100 magazines, 15,000+ websites, several research journals, college text books, newspapers, podcasts, and radio shows.

He was awarded as being one of the Top 40 Under 40 Business Professionals as well as being part of the Supplement Expert Panel.

Matt graduated from Penn State University with a degree in Kinesiology and a minor in Business back in 2005 but has been on a mission to make America healthy way before that. He is a certified strength and conditioning specialist, certified personal trainer, certified sports nutritionist, and is the owner of Weik Fitness and Writing Rebels.

Matt Weik has been active in the fitness industry and changing lives since 2002. He was also a DJ working for a well known radio station associated with CBS.

Read more at www.weikfitness.com.